Edwin Lassetter Bynner

The Chase of the Meteor

And Other Stories

Edwin Lassetter Bynner

The Chase of the Meteor
And Other Stories

ISBN/EAN: 9783337006297

Printed in Europe, USA, Canada, Australia, Japan

Cover: Foto ©Thomas Meinert / pixelio.de

More available books at **www.hansebooks.com**

THE

CHASE OF THE METEOR

AND OTHER STORIES

BY

EDWIN LASSETTER BYNNER

AUTHOR OF

"AGNES SURRIAGE," "PENELOPE'S SUITORS" "THE BEGUM'S
DAUGHTER," ETC.

WITH ILLUSTRATIONS BY F. T. MERRILL

BOSTON
LITTLE, BROWN, AND COMPANY
1891

PREFACE.

THIS little book, made up of stories from time to time contributed to "St. Nicholas," "Harper's Young People," the "Wide Awake," etc., is here offered as a holiday dish of junkets to all boys and girls, alike the good and the naughty, with a "Merry Christmas" from their constant friend the author.

Courtesies from Messrs. Harper and Brothers, and D. Lothrop and Company, in the matter of copyright, are gratefully acknowledged.

E. L. B.

Boston, 1891.

CONTENTS.

———◆———

LIST OF ILLUSTRATIONS.

I.

THE CHASE OF THE METEOR.

I.

THE CHASE OF THE METEOR.

THE down-train to Bellville had been gone an hour. The "accommodation" was ringing away from the station as Jake Handy, with a big piece of yellow soap in his hands, stood stooping over his little tin hand-basin, washing up to go home. It took a pretty lively scrubbing to get the soot and cinders all off, and Jake gave a little grunt of relief when it was done and he picked up the coarse jack-towel to dry himself. Then, having combed out his hair and beard before a triangular bit of looking-glass tacked up in the cab of the locomotive, he stood taking a critical look at the sky as he settled his greasy old cap on his head preparatory to starting.

"Looks kinder squally, but I guess 't won't rain 'fore I git back; but ef it does, you can let down the flap an' shet yourself in."

This was said to his son Dave, who sat on the bench by his side, and who had come down to "'tend the ingine," as he called it, while his father went for his supper.

"Mind, now, an' look out for the fire," continued the latter, opening the door and taking a farewell peep into the furnace; " you 'll hev to chuck in some more feed pooty soon, I guess. P'raps Jim 'll be back in time to tend to it, but don't depend on him."

Jim was the stoker, who had also gone to his supper; so that when Jake swung himself down to the track and disappeared in the darkness, Dave was left all alone in charge of the locomotive. But Dave was used to it; he was n't a bit afraid, and he knew every valve, wheel, and piston of the Meteor better than he did the doors and windows of his own house. Dave was only fifteen years old, but he had been accustomed to ride with his father on the locomotive ever since he could walk; so that Jake used to say, jocosely, " The little chap knows more 'bout it 'n I do." Dave indeed did know a good deal about it, and his father had frequently let him run the Meteor on long stretches of straight road where there was no chance of accident. He understood perfectly all the workings of the machinery, knew when to feed the fire, when to let off steam, how to back and go ahead, how to speed and slow up, to sound the whistle and ring the bell. It is not strange, therefore, that his father felt quite safe in leaving him in charge while he went off to get his supper. Besides, this was the regular thing every night. Jake Handy was the engineer of the "night freight." He got to Blankton at about eight o'clock in the evening, and had to " wait over," for two hours or more, until

the track was clear; then he could switch back
upon the main track and start off on his long night
course westward. During the time while he thus
lay upon the side track three trains usually passed,
— the Bellville Through Train, the Accommodation
to Dotville Junction, and last the Lightning Express. All this happened very conveniently for
Jake, for he lived at Blankton, and he was thus
able to go home and get a good hot supper every
night, instead of eating out of a tin pail, as he did
at dinner. If Jake had known, however, what was
going to happen while he was gone that night, you
may be sure he never would have budged a step.
As it was, he went whistling off through the darkness, thinking only of the kindly welcome and
comfortable supper awaiting him at home. It was
not quite nine o'clock when he left, the Lightning
was not due until ten, so that he had a good hour
and more to be gone.

As Jake had said, the sky looked "kinder
squally;" big black, dishevelled clouds were tossed
tumultuously all over it. The wind had sprung up,
and began to whistle ominously down the long,
dreary stretch of track beyond the freight-yard.
Fitful gusts tossed the dry leaves and rattled the
gravel against the sides of the Meteor. At first
Dave paid no attention; he let down the flap,
which was a kind of canvas curtain to shield
the engineer and fireman in stormy weather, and
pinned it securely in at the sides, thus making a

little snuggery of the cab; and then bringing forth a story-book which was tucked behind the leather cushion, he curled himself up on the stoker's seat and began to read.

But he did not remain long at peace. The wind grew every minute louder and fiercer. It tore off and swept away the flap which Dave had so carefully pinned down. It howled up and down the track, and in and out among the cars, rattling the coal in the tender, clanking the chains of the couplings, and making the fire under the boiler roar like mad.

The scene of this little story, it should be said, is out on the plains, where they have furious windstorms, and Dave was quite used to them; but when the gale reached such a pitch that it shook the train and ripped from the old tool-house whole clapboards and shingles, Dave began to look a little nervous, and glanced anxiously down the track to see if he could catch a glimpse of the two brakemen. But they were far away, quite at the other end of the long train, in the conductor's car, where they were cosily taking their supper before the little stove, and far out of reach of Dave's voice. The young engineer therefore thought to banish his anxiety by occupying himself about the locomotive.

"I guess I'll give her some supper," he said, opening the furnace-door and throwing in a few shovels of coal.

As he was in the act of doing this, suddenly, close at hand, there was heard a startling crash, and the next moment Dave saw a huge object sweep past him in the gloom, which to his dismay he recognized as the roof of the switch-house. Then he knew a tornado was upon them.

Although greatly alarmed, he did not lose his presence of mind; he kept his thoughts and attention fixed upon the Meteor, and busied himself in watching the steam-gauge and keeping up the fire, which the wind fanned into furious combustion. His anxiety, however, made the time seem very long; and before half an hour had elapsed he had already begun to listen nervously for his father's returning footsteps.

But now there comes a lull in the storm. Hark! what is that? Can it be the wind? No; it sounds more like distant thunder. Yet it cannot be thunder, for thunder is not continuous. It seems to come from afar off up the track, — it increases, it approaches.

Dave listens with his heart in his mouth. There is no mistake; above the shrieking and whistling of the wind this low, dull, ominous sound comes clearer, comes nearer and more near.

What can it be? Dave knows that no train is due from that direction. Straining his eyes, he looks far off up the level, curveless track; but no gleam of head-light, no spark of locomotive, dispels the dead blackness of the night. Another moment of suspense, and here at last it comes, — the track rattling, the very earth shaking under it, — a long, dark, sinuous object speeding down the track. 'T is here! 't is gone! With a roar like that of reverberating thunder, it shoots past the Meteor, and is out of sight in a minute.

Then at last the truth flashed upon Dave : *it was a runaway train!*

"A runaway train?" Yes, — a train without a locomotive, a train which starts itself, and having no brakeman aboard, no human hand to guide or restrain it, rushes on to its own destruction and that of everything in its path.

Dave had often heard his father tell stories of runaway trains, — what terrible things they were, and what frightful havoc they caused; but he had never seen one before. He knew directly whence this one had come. It was the coal-train from Dotville Junction, — eight big, heavy trucks loaded with coal, which his father had left the day before on a side-track to be unloaded. They had been started by the wind, and in twenty-four miles of down grade had acquired a fearful impetus.

For a moment Dave was paralyzed. Then suddenly he thought of the Lightning Express. In less than an hour it would be due. It could not be fifty miles away at that very moment, — fifty miles away, and coming toward them with the swiftness of the wind. It would surely collide with the runaway. Blankton was not a telegraph-station; there

was no way of warning the Lightning; there seemed
no earthly power to prevent the collision.

Forgetful, then, of the storm, of the danger, of
his own youth and inexperience, forgetful of everything but the frightful calamity impending over so
many sleeping, unconscious human beings, Dave
changed in a moment from a poor little shabby
engineer-boy to a hero, — as genuine a hero as
Leonidas, or Alexander, or Hannibal.

Jumping out of the locomotive, he called frantically to the brakemen. Again and again he
shouted, without avail; the wind drowned his
voice. Meanwhile time was flying; every moment
might cost a human life. Hesitating no longer,
Dave darted to the coupling, unshackled the Meteor,
sprang aboard, ran out across the switch upon the
main track, and set off in pursuit.

The runaway had already several miles the start
of him, and driven by the wind and its own impetus, was flying at fearful speed. But Dave had
the double advantage of wind and steam. He shov-
elled in the coal with nervous hands; and pulling
wide the throttle-valve, he stationed himself at the
outlook and shouted, " Go it, old girl!"

It would almost seem as if the Meteor understood both the command and the situation, as,
snorting and puffing and shrieking, she rushed like
a race-horse down the track.

Dave knew how much steam it was safe to carry;
and accordingly, with his eyes fixed upon the steam-

gauge, he spared not to push the engine to its top-most speed.

But all the time thoughts of the Lightning coming on filled him with dread. He did not know what o'clock it was; every minute seemed an hour. What would he not have given for a sight of his father, or of honest old Jim, the stoker! A strange, hollow feeling took possession of him; he felt himself grow light-headed at thought of the responsibility he had taken, as every minute increased the doubt and the danger.

Again and again, with his hand upon the throttle, he was upon the point of turning back; the runaway was possessed with the demon of speed, it seemed he could not overtake it, although the Meteor had never flown over the rails at such a rate before.

At last, just as, with trembling hand, he was about to reverse the throttle and give up the chase in good earnest, he rounded a curve in the road; and there, lo and behold! only a short distance before him, the long, dark hulk of the fugitive stood out in clear relief against the gravel of the road-bed. Dave's eyes gleamed again with hope: they had struck an up-grade in the road, and he was gaining upon them now with every minute.

Hereupon there presented itself a new problem. At his present rate of speed he must inevitably run into the coal cars with a crash. He must slow up, but do it so nicely and so carefully that when he did come up with them there should be the least possible shock. A sudden thought flashed through his mind: he had nobody to help him "couple." Overcome for the moment with dismay, he presently resolved to make the attempt himself. He little thought what a formidable task it was until he set about it.

Meantime, on he flew, revolving the situation in his head, and regulating his speed with the nicest care, until he was upon the very heels of the runaway. Then, holding on with might and main, he slipped out of the cab, and crawling along the side of the locomotive, at last clambered down upon the cow-catcher. Here, grasping the long coupler in one hand, and steadying himself with the other, he stood awaiting with breathless interest the approaching collision. The situation was perilous in the extreme: a gust of wind might sweep him from his place; he might be shaken off by the shock of contact, or crushed between the colliding bodies.

What wonder he was panic-stricken; what wonder that he turned back more than once from the dismaying task! To his startled ears the air seemed full of uncanny sounds, — the sweep of another tornado, the rush of the Lightning just ahead. That in the face of all these real and imaginary dangers he should have persevered in his purpose proves that he had in him the stuff of which heroes are made. The hero — let every boy and girl of you remember — is not he who is insensible to fear, but rather he who feels and realizes, but yet overcomes it.

Meantime the Meteor drew nearer and nearer to the flying train. The event showed that Dave had used excellent judgment in regulating its speed; for when it at last came up with the rear car, it was with scarcely a perceptible shock, so that although they were both going swiftly along, Dave was able quite comfortably to reach over and drop in the shackling-pin. Then, clambering back into the cab, with trembling eagerness he seized the throttle and very slowly and gradually reversed the engine. To his amazement, the train did not stop. Instead of the Meteor's stopping the run-away, the runaway dragged the Meteor along in its headlong flight. Dave was horror-stricken. He had thought, of course, that the train would stop at once. He had not counted upon the tremendous impetus all those heavy cars had acquired.

Now then began the tussle for mastery. Dave put on more steam. He talked to the Meteor as if she had been intelligent. He urged, he coaxed, he implored her to do her best. For a while it seemed all in vain; the puffing, struggling locomotive was dragged ignominiously along in the wake of the captured cars.

But Dave kept up the struggle. He put the Meteor to her mettle: nobly she strove, and nobly at last she won. The train presently began to slow up. Finally, after what seemed to Dave a short eternity, they came to a standstill. Thereupon began the backward pull. Slowly, very slowly, they got under way ; but once started, soon acquired momentum. But now, having the wind and much of the way, an up-grade, against them, their speed was nothing to what it had been in the other direction.

Meantime old fears gave way to new. The Lightning must be due by this time. Dave kept a sharp lookout behind, and whistled like mad around the curves, until, after many windings, he entered upon the long, straight stretch of road which extended in an unbroken line to Blankton. It was the home-stretch, — a good ten-mile run.

Dave heaved a long, deep sigh of relief ; but as it proved, he congratulated himself too soon, for the next moment he heard far behind, but this time unmistakably, the scream of the Lightning's whistle. Casting a terrified glance ahead, he measured the distance still to be run. He could not hasten, — he was going already at his utmost speed. He was making at most not more than forty miles an hour, while the Lightning was coming on at the rate of sixty. The next whistle sounded much nearer. With horror he realized how fast it was gaining on him. Hardly had he traversed two thirds of the remaining distance when the far-off gleam of its headlight came shooting round a wooded curve in his rear.

And now for a moment conflicting emotions almost overmastered him, — the nearness of the goal on one hand, the nearness of certain destruction on the other! It was a great crisis. Strange to say, out of the very despair of the moment Dave gathered calmness. He turned his back on the pursuing train; he cast no look behind; he shut his ears to its on-coming roar; he looked only straight ahead, keeping his eye fixed on the track, his mind fixed on his duty. On, on he flies. He comes nearer and nearer — he is there. Whistling furiously, he dashes past the station-house, across the switch, and down upon the side track.

It is all right, — Jake and Jim are there; they throw the switch back just in time, and the Lightning goes whizzing and shrieking past.

The next minute Jake jumps aboard the Meteor, and his gallant son faints dead away in his arms.

II.

JAMMER'S GHOST.

II.

JAMMER'S GHOST.

I NEED not tell you that Paul Apfelbaum was a German boy, — you will know that at once from the name; and all you boys and girls who have studied German will know furthermore that in English his name means Paul Appletree, — which sounds rather absurd, to be sure, but not a bit more absurd than ever so many English names.

Paul, however, did not care a snap what his name meant in English, or whether it meant anything at all. He was too wretched; in fact, he was the most dismal and unhappy little boy you ever saw or heard of. And what wonder! Almost every dreadful thing that could happen to a boy had happened to Paul, and all before he was fourteen years old. His father and mother had died years and years ago, before he was old enough to know them, and now his old grandmother, who had brought him up from a baby, had just died; so that he was not only left all alone in the big city of Hanover, but, worse still, apprenticed to a cross old instrument-maker whom all the neighbors called " Sauerkraut Johann," on account of his bad temper. Paul, however, had one friend. Yes, on the big round earth he had still left one faithful friend, and that friend was Jammer. To be sure, Jammer — Paul called it Yammer — was only a dog; but nevertheless he was far dearer than anything else in the world to his master. The feeling was mutual too; it dated back to the day when Paul rescued Jammer from a cruel cartman who was about to throw him into the river with a stone hung to his neck. Jammer, — Paul gave him that name, which means "misery," on account of his own and the dog's forlorn and friendless condition, — be it said, seemed entirely to understand the great obligation he owed to his master, for he repaid him with a wealth of gratitude and devotion which was the one solace of poor Paul's life.

Old Johann, of course, could n't bear the sight of Jammer, and drove him out of the shop with sticks and curses whenever he timidly ventured in. His master therefore had no resource but to keep him tied up in an old box at the end of the yard, where, it is to be feared, he often went hungry, although Paul conscientiously shared with the beast his own meagre rations. Then, when old Johann had fallen asleep over his mug of beer and his big brown meerschaum pipe, Paul stole down into the yard, released the poor brute, and together they wandered off in the moonlight up and down the city streets.

Meanwhile, as time wore on, matters grew worse with " Sauerkraut Johann ; " his eyes were getting dim, and his hands were getting stiff, so that he could no longer work as aforetime. People more-over were growing very tired of his sharp tongue and his surly looks, and the consequence was his business sadly fell off. This only made him more cross-grained than ever, and he vented his chagrin more and more on poor Paul.

It is said, however, that even a worm will turn ; and accordingly it chanced that one night as he was walking along, talking to his dog, Paul sud-denly broke out, —

" It's no use, Jämmerchen ; I can't stand it any longer. We must run away ! "

Jammer gave such an instant and emphatic bark of approval that Paul stooped over and hugged him.

" Ah ! if I only knew somewhere to go to, where old Johann couldn't find us. Grandmother said that Aunt Carlotta lived in America, in a great city called New York, and that she was rich and kind-hearted, and that when I grew up I must go to her ; but America, the good Father knows, is far, far away, quite at the other side of the world. We could never get there, never ! "

Jammer hung his tail in dejection.

" Besides, it would cost a great deal of money, and we have no money, not a pfennig. Ah, stay ! There is my little geldbeutel ; there may be money in that, but — "

Paul stopped, and looked down in doubt at Jammer. Jammer wagged his tail encouragingly.

" But," continued Paul, " Grandmother said I must never open that until things were at the worst. How, then," he concluded, violently stamping his foot, and dashing his cap to the ground, — " how, tell me, could they be worse ? "

Jammer barked so loudly and emphatically in response to this bold sentiment that Paul went on with more courage.

" I will do it ! Grandmother herself would bid me."

Stripping open his jacket without further ado, Paul pulled from his bosom a little leather purse which was suspended from his neck by a cord. Naturally he hesitated a moment before opening it. His grandmother had given it to him on her deathbed, charging him solemnly not to open it except in some moment of need or suffering. The moment at length seemed to have come which his grandmother herself would have regarded as a crisis.

Pressing the spring, therefore, he opened the purse, and beheld within three golden double-Friedrichs. He almost swooned with joy. Three double-Friedrichs, and all his own ! He could scarcely contain himself. Never in his life had he possessed one before. Taking them reverently in his hand, he held them up in the blaze of the street-lamp for closer inspection ; then, at the sound of approaching footsteps, he thrust them hastily back in the purse and ran away. Three gold pieces! How the bright vision haunted his dreams all the night long! He beheld the little geldbeutel swell to enormous proportions; he saw it filled with a shining mass of gold pieces, — they were all his own.

It was a great shock to wake up in the morning and find himself lying on his rude pallet under the eaves, with the sound of old "Sauerkraut Johann's" big stick knocking on the wall for him to get up.

Next day, as he was hurrying along the street on an errand for old Johann, he saw an advertisement which said in big letters : —

AMERICA !

Notice to Emigrants.

NEW YORK AND HANOVER STEAMSHIP Co.

Cheap Steerage Rates!

Steamers sail every Wednesday and Saturday.

Something prompted Paul to go in. Before he knew what he was doing, he found himself at the counter, asking a gruff-looking clerk with big moustache, "How much will it cost to take a boy to America ?"

"Sixteen dollars; and you'd better take passage at once if you want to go."

"Yes, I suppose so," said Paul, hesitatingly.

"Next steamer?" asked the clerk.

"I — I — didn't mean — I only wanted to ask a question," stammered Paul.

"Eh!" roared the fierce clerk, "you don't want to go, after putting me to this trouble ?"

"Ye-es, yes, I do ; I think I will."

"Very well, then," concluded the clerk, going on with his writing, "count out your money."

Paul, trembling with misgiving as to the results of the step he was about to take, fished out the little geldbeutel and handed over the precious coin.

Paul went home trembling with excitement. The great step was taken. It was too late now to draw back ; he must go to America. Night and day he could think of nothing else. Accordingly, he made so many blunders in his work that old Johann beat him more than ever.

But Paul cared nothing for a beating now ; the day of deliverance was near at hand. He confided to Jammer his hopes and fears, and bided his time. At length Wednesday morning came. Paul was up early, and attended to his duties as usual. About noon old Johann fortunately sent him out to mail a letter. Little did the old instrument-maker think, as he shouted after him, "Be quick, now, you lazy rascal!" — little did he suspect, I say, that he would never see his apprentice again.

Posting the letter as quickly as possible, Paul stole round to the back gate, where he had left his clothes done up in a neat parcel, and quietly untying Jammer, he turned his back forever upon old "Sauer-

kraut" and his gloomy shop, and made the best of
his way to the ship. Here a great shock awaited
him. As he was about going up the gang-plank
leading to the deck, closely followed by the faithful
Jammer, a rough voice shouted, —

"Here! what are you about? Drive off that
dog!"

"No, no," cried Paul, eagerly, — "that is Jammer; that is my dog. He is going over the sea
to America."

"Over the sea! He'll go *under* the sea if you
don't get him away from here pretty quick. No
dogs allowed on board this ship. Off with him, I
say!" shouted the officer.

Paul was aghast. Leave Jammer? Leave behind the only friend he had in the world? Never!
He took the faithful dog in his arms and carried
him down the plank to the crowded pier. What
could he do? Must he lose his chance of going
to America? Must he lose his money, — those
precious gold pieces which his grandmother had
left to rescue him from poverty and suffering?
Must he go back to "Sauerkraut Johann" to be
beaten and cursed for the rest of his life? These
questions whirled through poor Paul's brain, and
found no answer. Holding tight hold of Jammer,
he sat down on a huge packing-box on the outskirts
of the crowd and fairly wept. An old woman was
arranging her fruit-stall close at hand, and presently saw him.

"What is the matter, younker?" said she.
"Cry? A boy cry? Pooh! it is for girls and
babies to cry, because they are silly fools. What
is the matter?"

Paul dried his eyes and stated his case.

"And is that all?" asked the old woman, laughing. "You must have plenty of tears if you can
waste them over such trifles. For me, I would
not cry."

"What would *you* do?" asked Paul, eagerly.

"I would go to America, and I would take my
dog. That man there, he is a brute; he makes not
the rules; 't is none of his business. 'No dogs on
the ship?' Pooh! Put a gold piece in his hand,
and you might take a dozen."

"But I am not rich, and I have no gold piece."

"Then if you have no money, you ought to have
wit, which will do just as well sometimes. Listen
to me. You see that old fruit-basket, — it is stout
and strong. Put in your dog and your parcel too,
tie this piece of canvas over the top, and carry it
aboard, and who is the wiser, tell me?"

Paul stared at this bold proposition. He was
startled to think of such cool defiance of authority.

"Come," said the old woman, "you'd better be
making up your mind, my lad. See, they have the
freight nearly all aboard, and in a few minutes the
ship will be off."

Just then Jammer uttered a low, appealing whine;
it seemed to say, "Do not leave me." This decided

the matter. Paul pointed to the basket, the dog jumped in directly, as though he had understood the whole conversation. Paul tucked in his small parcel of clothes, and then, cautioning Jammer not to bark or make a sound, he spread the canvas over all, and, aided by the old woman, tied it down securely with a stout cord.

"Here," continued the latter, "I'll lend you a hand; it's too heavy for you to carry by yourself. Let us see if yonder busybody will dare to say any-thing to me!"

Paul was greatly reassured by this sympathy and assistance, and poured out his thanks to the old woman.

"Tush! Wipe your face! You'll never be a man till you get over being a baby. Here!" she cried to a boy standing near, "mind my stand while I am gone. See you eat no fruit now, and you shall have an orange when I come back."

Taking hold of the basket, the two quickly made their way up the plank, the old woman boldly elbowing past the very officer who had forbidden Paul to bring his dog aboard. Going below to the place assigned to the steerage passengers, Paul deposited the basket under his bunk and bade good-by to the old woman, offering her a few pen-nies for her basket, which she was too business-like to refuse.

In a few minutes more they were off, and Paul breathed freer; but for days he was constantly

haunted with anxiety lest Jammer should be discovered. When night came, he would let him out
of the basket, and occasionally during certain hours
of the day when there was least danger of discovery.
His fellow-passengers in the steerage of course
soon learned the facts of the case, and warmly
sympathized with Paul, promptly giving him warning whenever an officer approached. Thus, as
every day seemed to diminish the danger, Paul
gradually grew to feel more at ease; indeed, he
had almost ceased to have any anxiety at all in the
matter, when one day, on returning to his bunk, he
found Jammer missing. His bunk, the basket, the
whole steerage quarters, were searched in vain.
Paul became nearly frantic; he rushed wildly
hither and thither, telling his loss and asking the
passengers if they had seen Jammer. But nobody
had seen him. Paul was in despair. Just at this
moment a great uproar arose in the cook's galley,
and directly the cook himself appeared, with a very
red face and wrathful look, dragging by the neck
a dog, in whose mouth was a huge piece of meat;
it was Jammer. Paul stood stupefied; he could
hardly believe his eyes. Jammer guilty of theft?
Alas! poor beast, it was too true. Hunger had
overcome prudence, honor, obedience, — all the
higher dog morals. The smell of cooking meat
had tempted him from the bunk; he had stolen
unobserved to the cook's galley, and when that
person's back was turned, he had seized the piece

of meat, and was about making off when he was discovered and captured.

The angry cook now dragged the guilty Jammer toward the side of the vessel. His intention was evident. Paul rushed frantically forward to interfere.

"Oh, don't, don't! He didn't mean to. He was hungry. He didn't know it was your meat!"

"Stand off, or I will throw *you* over after him!" shouted the enraged cook.

"Stop! stop! it is my Jammer; it is all I have in the world. See, I will pay you; I will give you all my money if —"

"It is too late," cried the cook, throwing the struggling dog far over the ship's side into the foaming waves. "Now get you gone, or I will serve you the same."

Sick with grief and horror, Paul took one last look at his darling Jammer as the latter rose to the surface of the water and began swimming frantically after the ship, and then rushed off to his bunk, where he threw himself down in a passionate fit of weeping.

The rest of the voyage was a blank to poor Paul. The future was all darkness. He shuddered at the thought of that strange country to which he was going, where everybody would speak in an unknown tongue, where nobody would know him. Perhaps his aunt was no longer living; perhaps she would care nothing for him. He wished himself back in

Hanover; he wished himself at the bottom of the sea with poor Jammer.

At last they arrived in New York harbor. Despite his sadness, Paul gazed with curiosity and interest at the tall buildings, at the forest of shipping, at the many strange sights of a foreign city. Meantime the ship approached its dock. Immediately all was noise and bustle. Dock-hands and stevedores and 'longshoremen and porters and hack-drivers all jostled each other in the crowd, shouting and crying and making an indescribable din and confusion.

Paul looked down upon the noisy scene in dismay. This, then, was the New World, and he must go down into it and make his way alone in it. The thought made him homesick. He would far rather have stayed on board the ship. The ship had begun to feel like home to him a little. He was at length startled from his musing by a voice behind him, saying, —

" Come, younker, this is America."

Paul started, and saw with astonishment that he was the last passenger left upon the ship. He hastened to get his parcel and follow. Going down the steep gang-plank to the dock, he looked around him with a dazed feeling, quite at a loss where to go or what to do. Standing thus, his attention was attracted by a dog which stood on the dock facing him and wagging its tail. Paul rubbed his eyes. What a strange, what a wonderful resemblance !

"Good Heaven! It is Jammer's ghost!"

" Bist du hier, Jammer ? " (Are you here, Jammer), gasped Paul.

To his amazement the dog, on hearing these words, bounded forward, and leaped upon him with delight, barking, and licking his hands and face.

Paul dropped his parcel, his eyes almost started from their sockets, his mouth fell open, his hair rose.

" Mein lieber Himmel ! es ist Jammer's Geist ! " (Good Heaven ! it is Jammer's ghost !), he cried, and fell over backward in a swoon.

Many of his fellow-passengers were standing on the dock, and rushed to his assistance. It was a long time before he came to his senses, and even then he seemed light-headed, and talked a little wild. Moreover, on seeing the dog again, he became very much excited, and trembled at its approach. The story spread far and near among the emigrants of the appearance of the ghost dog. Many of Paul's fellow-passengers came to look at Jammer's ghost, and were almost as much terrified as Paul himself. Some said it must be a ghost, while others stoutly maintained that it was Jammer himself.

The strange story at last came to the ears of a young Frenchman who had just arrived from Havre on the French ship " Marguerite." He made his way to the spot, saw the dog, and thereupon told the following marvellous story : —

" Zat dog! My faith! do I know him? Yes.

Ve find him in ze ocean. Attend! You shall hear. Ve had beau temps, — a fine day. Ze sun shine, ze vind blow, everyzing magnifique, ven: ' Stop! Arrest yourself,' say some one. Vat is it? Aha! ze ter-r-rible ber-rgs of ice. One, two, tree — a douzaine. Behold ze situation! Vat to do? Ze capitaine he 'ave ze great 'ead, sublime sense, an' ze heart of a lion. Vat he do? He stand still. See ze effect. Ze ber-rgs, ven zey see ve shall not come to be crush, sail avay, far avay out of ze view. But vile ve vait somezing arrive to us. Ve see a spectacle remarkable. Somezing move in ze vater. Nobody know him. Vere comes he from? He see us; he try to come to us. Ve peek him up. Behold! it ees a dog; but, my faith! no more but half alive. Vere he come from? Vere he go to? Nobody can say. It is a thing extraordinaire. Ve make him dry, an' bring him to zees place, and straightavay ve loose him. He vanish. Ve hear ze story of ze ghost. Ve come, and behold it is again our dog of ze sea."

" What time did the ' Marguerite ' get in?" asked one of the officers of the German ship.

" Zees morning, to-day," returned the Frenchman.

" At what o'clock?" asked the officer again.

" Ten o'clock, — two, tree hours ago."

" That's it," said the German. " We threw the dog overboard and you picked him up. The ' Marguerite ' is a faster ship than the ' Kaiserblumen ;' you passed us in the night, and arrived here first,"

" Yonder-rful ! " ejaculated the Frenchman.

" Does this dog belong to you ? " asked the officer of Paul, who stood by in dumb amazement.

" Ye-es, no ; if — if — Do you think it can be Jammer ? "

" Call him and see," said the officer.

Paul called, and Jammer, overjoyed to hear once more the familiar voice, sprang upon him with delight.

" How came you to have a dog on board ? " asked the officer again.

With doubt and hesitation Paul told how he had smuggled Jammer aboard the ship. The officer happily was touched by the tale and by Paul's friendless and forlorn condition, and told him, greatly to his surprise and delight, that he and Jammer could stay on board the " Kaiserblumen " until he found his aunt.

Paul gratefully availed himself of the invitation and it only remains to add that in the course of a week, by means of the publication of the story of Jammer's escape in all the papers, Aunt Carlotta heard of the arrival of her nephew, and hurrying post-haste to the " Kaiserblumen," gave both him and Jammer a hearty welcome.

III.

THE EXTRA TRAIN.

III.

THE EXTRA TRAIN.

CHAPTER I.

THE SECRET.

YOU'D better believe I was glad when that letter came from Uncle Joe; for Mother and Father had promised me that if I should get a good average in my marks at school, I might go and spend the vacation at Uncle Joe's. I put in and studied like a Trojan, and at the end of the term I stood third in my class. Jim Stearns and Wally Lyon were ahead of me; but Jim is sixteen, and Wally's mother helps him at home. At any rate, Father and Mother were satisfied, and that's all I cared for.

But about Uncle Joe's letter. Oh, wasn't I glad! Uncle Joe is a splendid man; I was named after him, and he always calls me Young Joe. He lives in Massachusetts, and is President of a Railway Company. He said in the letter that I must be sure to come, for he was going to take us young ones away somewhere to have a good time all summer.

As luck would have it, school was just over when the letter came. 1 was measured for a new roughing suit of clothes, Father bought me a stunning fishing-rod and tackle, and I squeezed in my baseball and bats after Mother had packed my trunk, — 1 had to laugh when 1 saw how she had put all the socks and handkerchiefs in little rows and piles. I thought they would n't stay that way a great while. And right on the top of all I put the presents I had bought for Cousin Hal and Susy and Baby Bunting. At last I started. I went by the Fall River boat, and Father stood on the pier waving his handkerchief until we were out of sight.

Cousin Hal met me at the train the next morning when I got out. They were all real glad to see me, and Aunt Maria had a tip-top breakfast. Hal's school had closed the day before; but Uncle Joe said we should not start off on our trip until the next week, so we should have two or three days to knock around in.

It was a great secret where we were going. Hal did n't know, Susie did n't know; and when we asked any questions, Uncle Joe had a funny twinkle in his eye, and Aunt Maria laughed. They said it was n't to the seaside, nor to the mountains, nor to a hotel, nor to a boarding-house, nor on a ship, nor in a tent. At last Susie guessed "up in a balloon," and everybody laughed; but Uncle Joe shook his head again, and so we gave up guessing.

That was on Sunday night, just before we went upstairs. Hal went down, when he was half undressed, to ask if it was in a cave; and when his father said "No," Hal said, then it could n't be anywhere. We went to bed at nine o'clock, for we were going to start early the next morning.

Hal and I were up before anybody else. We could n't eat much breakfast, in spite of all that Aunt Maria said. We had a good many things to see to. Hal was going to take his dog, Susie her canary, and Baby Bunting a pet rabbit, which we carried in a box. Uncle Joe said it was a regular menagerie.

We went down to the depot in two carriages, with a lumber wagon behind to carry all the baggage. We had hardly got there, when the train came along. We had a whole car to ourselves; and as Uncle Joe is the president, of course we were "passed," and the conductor did n't come around to take our tickets. So Hal made believe he was the conductor, and put a badge on his hat, and went up and down the aisle, calling out at every step, "Tickets, please!" and Baby Bunting gave him a bit of card, and it tickled Baby Bunting 'most to death.

We went through a good many towns and places, but we did n't stop, except once to "water up." It was past noon, when all at once we "slowed up," in a wild sort of place out in the woods, and pretty soon we began to back. We backed and backed as much as a quarter of a mile, on a side-track, until we came to a place that was all woods on one side, and clear, open fields upon the other; and then we stopped. We asked Uncle Joe what it meant; but he told us to keep still, and we should see very soon; and then he got up and went out and talked with the engineer and brakemen. We could n't hear what they said; but pretty soon the engine went off and left us. We told Aunt Maria, and she laughed again, but said nothing.

By and by, Uncle Joe came back and said:

"Now, youngsters, come with me!"

We all jumped up and followed him in Indian file. He went out and unlocked the door of the next car and told us to go in. We rushed past him into the car and stopped, and all cried, —

"Oh!"

What do you think it was? Why, the car was made into a parlor, — not a Pullman palace-car, but a regular parlor, such as we have at home. All the seats had been taken out; there was a carpet on the floor, there were the sofa and easy-chairs from Aunt Maria's room put around the wall, there was the piano at one side, there was a centre-table and some shelving for books, — just like a room at home.

We asked Uncle Joe lots of questions; but he only smiled, and again said, "Come along!" and went on to the next car. Then we all shouted again, for that was fixed up for three sleeping-rooms, — one for Uncle Joe and Aunt Maria, at one end, a little one in the middle for Susie and Baby Bunting, and then one at the other end for Hal and me. There were six little iron beds, and all the rooms were divided off with heavy curtains; and there were funny little wash-stands, and combs and brushes, and lots of nails to hang our clothes on, and it was just the jolliest thing you ever saw!

Then Uncle Joe led us into the next car, and there was a dining-room, — a large table in the middle, a lot of chairs, and a cupboard up in the corner with plenty of crockery.

As soon as we saw that, we all clapped our hands and cried out, —

"Oh! now we know the secret: we are going to live in the cars all summer!"

Uncle Joe smiled, and looked at Aunt Maria.

"But where's the kitchen?" cried Susie. "Are we going to cook out of doors?"

Uncle Joe did n't answer, but went to the door and beckoned, and there was another car! And when we went in, we found it was a splendid kitchen; and there sat our own cook and second girl from home, laughing and kind of blushing to see us rush in. They had a nice little bed-room partitioned off for them at the farther end of the car; but when Aunt Maria asked them how they liked it, we all laughed to hear the cook answer, —

"Shure, 'tis very nate an' foine, ma'am, but

4

we'd be sheared out of our lives wid the wild bastes and Injuns."

"Now, pickaninnies," said Uncle Joe, when we went out, "this is to be your home for the summer!"

We shouted with delight; Hal and I threw up our hats, Susie danced a little jig, Baby Bunting flourished his fat little arms, and altogether we made so much noise that Aunt Maria begged us to stop.

"This is to be our summer home," said Uncle Joe, again. "And now the question is, what shall we call it?"

"Let's call it 'The Sportsman's Bower,'" cried Hal, thinking of his gun and fishing-rod.

"Or 'The Huntsman's Haunt,'" said I.

"Or 'The Railroad Ranch,'" cried Susie.

"Or 'The Travelling Troupe,'" said Hal.

"Or 'The Roving Roost,'" said I.

"Why not call it what it is," asked Uncle Joe, — "'The Extra Train'?"

We all thought that would be first-rate, and said: "Yes, let's have that!"

"Very well," said Uncle Joe. "I will have a sign painted, and send it down to-morrow when Bo's'n comes with the horse."

"Is Bo's'n coming? and the horse too? Oh, what fun!" cried Susie.

"Yes," said Uncle Joe.

"Where will they stay? There isn't any stable," suggested Hal.

"We shall have to build one," said his father.
" Let 's go out now and choose a spot."

We all went out and jumped off the car, and
then we saw what a beautiful place we were in.
It was very high ground. There was a mountain
not very far off on one side, and a little lake quite
near on the other. There was a splendid view;
we could see miles and miles away. There were
ever so many hills, — big hills too, — and lots of
towns and villages 'way, 'way off in the distance,
so that we could just see the spires of the churches.
Oh, I can't tell you how grand it was!

Uncle Joe told us that the track we were on
ran about a quarter of a mile farther to a gravel-pit,
but that it had not been used for several years, and
we should not be disturbed. He said, also, that
the cars were old cars that the company did n't
want any more, and that 's how he came to take
them. The engineer and brakemen had blocked
the wheels tight before they went away, so that
we could n't move. The track was not sandy, as
most railway tracks are, but the grass came clear
up to the rails, and the blackberry-vines ran all
over the sleepers in some places.

We hunted around for a spot in which to build
the stable, and Uncle Joe at last picked out one
in a little clump of trees, at one side of the big
open place. We left him drawing plans upon a
piece of paper while we ran and capered all over
the wide green pasture, which we named "The

Field," playing "Tag" and "Gule" and "Leap-
frog," till all at once Aunt Maria came out of the
dining-room car and stood on the steps ringing a
big bell. We wondered what it was for; but when
we went in we saw a splendid dinner ready, set
just as it is at home. We were glad to see it too,
for we were pretty hungry by that time.

After dinner, Uncle Joe said we should go out
and pitch the lawn-tent and mark out the tennis-
ground. We found a fine place; and after we had
got it measured off and arranged, Aunt Maria
came out to join us, and we played all the
afternoon.

After that there was the prettiest sunset I ever
saw: the lake was all gold, and the mountain deep
purple. But it seemed sort of solemn and dreary
at first, when the night came on, there were so
many queer sounds; for besides the crickets and
tree-toads there were lots of whippoorwills, and
something else, now and then, that Uncle Joe
said was a screech-owl. I couldn't help thinking
then of what the cook had said about the "wild
bastes an' Injuns;" but I didn't say anything to
Hal about it, for he would have laughed at me.

We forgot about the woods pretty quickly when
we went in; for Aunt Maria had the big astral
lamp lighted on the centre-table, and we had
games, and some music on the piano, and then we
thought it was great fun going to bed in those
droll little beds and bed-rooms. We knew noth-

ing after that until old Meg, the cook, rang a
tremendous big bell for us to get up in the
morning.

We did n't know where we were at first, but we
soon were dressed and out. And, oh! you never
saw anything so fresh and sweet as the woods
were, nor heard such a racket as the birds made.

We had breakfast pretty early, because Uncle
Joe was going away. We went with him down
to the main track ; he shook his handkerchief when
the train came along, and the engineer, who was
on the lookout, stopped and took him up.

That afternoon a car was switched off upon our
track by the "up" freight-train, with two carpenters and a lot of lumber on it. The carpenters
went right to work building the stable. It was a
rough-looking little shed when it was done; but it
was nice and warm inside, and it was hidden by
the trees, so its looks did n't matter. The carpenters stayed two days, and did a lot of little jobs for
Aunt Maria; they made some steps to go up into
the cars by, for the car-steps were too high to be
easy; then they made some benches to put around
in "The Field," where Aunt Maria could come
and sit to see us play, and where we could sit
when we were tired.

The day after the stable was done, Bo's'n came
with the horse. We were awful glad to see him.
You ought to have seen how he grinned when he
saw the stable and we told him about naming

"The Extra Train." Bo's'n is a real good-natured fellow; he is as strong as a giant almost, and knows how to do everything. His name is n't really Bo's'n, you know, — it is George Latham; but we call him Bo's'n because he was once a real boatswain on a great ship. He said he would show Hal and me how to snare rabbits and partridges in the woods, and teach us to swim and dive and float and a lot of things.

Aunt Maria said she felt more "to rights" after the carpenters had gone and Bo's'n had come; for she confessed she had been a little afraid before, though Hal said she need n't have been, for he had his shot-gun.

Bo's'n found a splendid spring in the woods, and used to bring the water every day in big buckets. Then he found an old grass-grown road by which we could drive the horse and carriage out to the highway; and then we used to take a long ride all round the country every day.

Uncle Joe came down 'most every night, and always brought a big basket of things from the city. That makes me think I have n't told you how we did our marketing.

Why, the morning train used to stop and drop it off in a big market-basket two or three times a week, and Bo's'n was down there to get it. The engineer soon knew the spot, and used to give us a salute whenever he went by, — a kind of "toot, toot," on the steam-whistle. We liked to hear it, but I guess the passengers in the cars thought it was funny.

Saturday night an engine came down on purpose to bring Uncle Joe, who had been kept by business too late to take the cars. Then Aunt Maria said, as long as the engine was there, she wanted the cars shifted so as to put the sleeping-car at the farther end from the kitchen, — which was a good deal better; for then we did n't have to go through "the sleeper" to get to the dining-room.

You know now pretty well what sort of a place we lived in, and so I 'll go on and tell you some of our adventures.

CHAPTER II.

"JIM CROW."

AFTER the first week we felt just as much at home on "The Extra Train" as in our own houses. Our papers and letters were thrown out of the cars every day by the expressman in a little canvas bag, and Hal and I went down the first thing in the morning to get it.

Uncle Joe took us down to the lake one day, and picked out the very prettiest boat there, and hired it for the season. Her name was "Undine," and she was the fastest boat on the lake. Bo's'n

rather turned up his nose at her at first, I think,
and said, —

"She's all well enough p'r'aps for *fresh
water.*"

She was nothing but a row-boat, of course; but
he fixed her up with a cat-rigging, and we used
to have some jolly sails in her.

Aunt Maria said it was a sweet little lake, and
so it was; and not so very little, for it was six
miles long.   We used to go fishing 'most every
day at first; we caught perch and horn-pouts, and
now and then a pickerel.   We took Baby Bunting
one day, and he actually caught a fish, — a funny
little flat fish, — and pulled it in with his own fat
little hands; and his eyes stuck out of his head
almost.

He took such care of that fish!   He wrapped it
up in a piece of paper, he put in his pocket, he
carried it home and took it to bed with him, and
cried as if his heart would break next day, when
Aunt Maria said it must be thrown away.   But he
stopped crying when we promised to get him some
more.   And so we did; we made a little aquarium
out in a hollow rock, and put in two or three
little fishes; but they didn't thrive, for Baby
Bunting would take them out and nurse them every
day, and squeeze them affectionately in his fat
little fists.

But speaking about the boat makes me think of
the first scrape we got into, — and it *was* a scrape,

I tell you. Everybody was scared 'most to death for a while. This is the way it happened: —

Aunt Maria said, the day before Hal's birthday, that we should have a huckleberry pudding next day for dinner if we would go and pick the berries.

Of course we were glad enough to do that; so, in the afternoon, Hal and Susie and I set out to go to the hills. But after we had gone about half a mile, Hal stopped all of a sudden and said he remembered seeing lots of huckleberries over on Crow Island, and we 'd better go there.

Crow Island is the biggest island in the lake, and it got its name from always having flocks of crows flying and cawing round it.

We thought it would be ever so much more fun to go to the island; so we got the "Undine" and rowed over. We found lots of berries, and picked our baskets heaping full. It was nearly sundown when we started to come home. We were just getting into the boat, when Susie pointed to a large pine-tree not far away in which the crows were making a great noise. We went round to see what it was, and discovered a big crow's nest near the top.

"I 'll bet there are some young ones up there!" I said.

"Come on, let 's go up, then!" cried Hal. "It would be such fun to have a young crow; we 'd teach him to talk."

Without another word we both started up the

tree. It was pretty hard climbing, and when we
got about half way up, the old crows began making
a horrible noise over our heads; but we climbed on,
up and up, until we were within reach of the nest.
There it was, sure enough, so full of young birds
that it was a wonder some of them did n't tumble
out.

The old crows made a great fight, and darted
right at our faces. Hal said he was afraid they 'd
pick out our eyes; and so was I. Worse than that,
we were up so very high that I was dizzy, and my
knees shook like everything. I kept hold, though,
like grim death. Hal shouted, —

"Brace right up, now, and don't go flunking!"

And I did n't. He kept the old ones off by
fighting them with his hat, while I grabbed a fine
young crow, and we scrambled down. I did n't
dare to look below, for I thought I should fall
every minute; and that young varmint of a crow,
— my goodness, did n't he caw and kick, though!
He opened his mouth as if he were going to swal-
low me, tree and all. He knew he was being kid-
napped, I can tell you. But Hal and I did n't feel
guilty, for we knew we were going to civilize that
crow and give him the advantage of an education;
and then, if he wanted to, he could go back as a
missionary to the other crows, you know. Any
way, we got down with him all right; and now
begins the scrape. Just as we reached the ground
we heard a cry from Susie. We ran toward the

lake, and what do you think? There was the boat with Susie in it out in the deep water, half a dozen rods from the shore, and Susie herself with one of the oars was paddling for dear life, and all the time only making the boat go round and round in a circle! She had been thrown into such a fright when she first found herself floating away from shore that she had lost overboard the other oar.

This was a pretty pickle; for Hal and I could only swim a few strokes then, and of course we could n't go 'way out there in that deep water. We made believe not to be scared, but we were; for the night was coming on, and we were left alone upon the island without any way of getting off. And there was the boat, with poor Susie in it crying as if her heart would break, floating off toward the farther end of the lake, from which she would have to walk miles and miles through the woods to get home. Besides all that, we knew Aunt Maria would be frightened within an inch of her life.

We shouted to Susie not to be afraid, but to sit still in the boat, and she would float ashore; and then Hal and I began calling and shouting and hooting, in the hope that somebody would hear us. And soon we were both as hoarse as frogs. But of course Aunt Maria thought we had gone toward the mountain, and she would hunt in that direction first, when she missed us.

But all this time poor Susie kept floating farther and farther off, until she looked like a big speck on the water; and the light was fading fast.

At last we saw somebody moving on the shore. We both tried to shout, but we were too hoarse to shout loudly.

Then what do you s'pose we did? Why, Hal stripped off his shirt, and we tied it to a tall pole by the sleeves, so as to make a white flag; and we waved it back and forth, taking turns at it until our arms ached.

Pretty soon we heard a voice calling. We tried to answer, but we couldn't make much of a noise; so we kept on waving the shirt. By and by the voice came nearer; but it was getting so dark that we couldn't see anything plainly. In a few minutes we heard the splashing of oars, and then came Bo's'n's voice calling us by name. We managed to make him hear us this time; and when he came up to the rock where we were, we both leaped into the boat and almost hugged him, we were so glad. He had brought along Tearer, Hal's dog, who nearly ate us up with delight, just as if he understood all about the scrape we had been in.

When we told Bo's'n about Susie he seemed a little scared at first; but in a minute he said, —

"Never you fear, she's all right, we'll git her; but we must give your ma the signal first, — she's

over there on the shore, an' she's e'en a'most
crazy. I told her ef' t was all right I'd signal."
And striking a match as he spoke, he lighted a
lantern in the bottom of the boat and swung it
round his head three times.

"There, that'll ease *her* mind, I reckon; an'
now we'll go after the little one!"

With that he just "lay to" the oars, as he called
it, and made the boat almost fly through the water
in the direction we showed him. Now and then
he stopped and wet his finger and stuck it up in
the air to see which way the wind blew. Then he
would change his course and row harder than
before. Hal and I were so anxious that we didn't
say much; but we kept a sharp lookout, and every
now and then I swung the lantern. It seemed as
if Bo's'n had rowed a tremendous distance, and
that he never would reach the other end of the
lake. We thought he had made a mistake in
changing his course; but he only said, —

"Now, you jest leave this 'ere to me, boys; you
jest leave this 'ere to me."

By and by we saw the dark shadow of the woods
on shore. We all shouted, —

"Susie! Susie!"

But not a sound came back excepting a kind of
echo from the woods. I kept swinging the lantern all the time, Hal was frightened nearly out of
his wits, and Tearer barked like a good fellow.

Hal and I were going to get out, but Bo's'n

stopped us; he said we could hunt better in the boat than on shore.

Then he rowed along shore, keeping well in, and pretty soon we saw some object in the bushes. We rowed up, and there, sure enough, was the " Undine," but — *she was empty!*

Oh, how scared Hal and I were! We could hardly breathe at first, and I felt all kind of hollow inside. We thought Susie was drowned; but Bo's'n kept saying, —

"Don't you be scared a bit; set right still here in the boat! I'll find her."

He jumped out and called the dog. Tearer went bounding into the woods, and we could hear him for a little while racing back and forth, this way and that, trying to find the scent. In a few minutes the sound of Bo's'n's footsteps and the barking both died away, and it was terribly still and dark and lonely.

We waited and waited and waited. It seemed as if 't was almost a year, and by and by, after a long, long time, we heard a shout; then Tearer's bark; then the crackling of the bushes; and pretty soon out came Bo's'n, with Susie in his arms. He came right on board, took off his coat and wrapped her in it, and put her down on the seat between Hal and me.

She acted in a very funny way at first. She laughed one minute and she cried the next; her teeth chattered, and she shivered all over. Bo's'n said he guessed she'd got "the histrikes" slightly, but she'd get over *them* quick enough when she got back to her ma.

We didn't lose much time in getting home, you can imagine; and there was poor Aunt Maria waiting on the shore in the greatest fright. I expected she would scold Hal and me, but she didn't. She hugged us and kissed us, and called us her dear children, and took us home and gave us a splendid supper, and was as kind as ever she could be. And she has never said a word about it since, nor forbidden us to go again, nor anything of the sort.

And I guess that was the best way, for Hal and I felt as bad as we could any way, and I think it would have been a sort of relief to be scolded. Instead of that, Aunt Maria was so awful good to us that it cut us up worse than ever.

And that was our first regular scrape; but I forgot to tell one thing. After we had reached home and we stood shivering around the fire, Aunt Maria said to me suddenly, —

"Why, my dear, what's that you have in your hand?"

I looked down, and there was the poor little crow which I had tied up in my handkerchief and carried all the time, without ever knowing it. He was all alive and well, in spite of what he had been through. We called him "Jim," in honor of the renowned "Jim Crow." We taught him a good many tricks, and he grew up to be a wonderful bird. I wish I had time to tell you some of the funny things he did.

CHAPTER III.

GOING UP THE MOUNTAIN.

NOW I must tell you about our trip up the mountain, for that was rather an exciting event, — at least we thought so.

We had been waiting ever so long to go, so at last Aunt Maria said one evening that we should start the next morning. It was a splendid day. We had an early breakfast. Aunt Maria packed a big basket with luncheon, and Bo's'n drove us over to the Mountain House, — a hotel right at the foot of the mountain, where we left the carriage.

There was a good path, so we thought there was no danger of losing the way, and it was easy going at first. Bo's'n carried Baby Bunting, and Hal and I carried the hamper. But pretty soon the way became steeper, and it got to be awfully hot. We all sat down in a shady place to get cool. We were so thirsty that we almost choked. While we sat there groaning for a drink, all at once Tearer, who had been dashing about in the woods, came rushing up to us.

"There! there! See that! he's found it!" shouted Bo's'n, and pointed at Tearer's feet.

We looked, and, sure enough, his feet were all wet. Then Hal and I jumped up, took a pail, and went hunting about in the woods with him; and there, about half a dozen rods from the path, we found a splendid brook.

The water was as cold as ice and as clear as crystal. We took back a pail of it. Aunt Maria said it was the best water she had ever tasted, and that we must stop there on the way down to get another drink.

Now, just that one remark of Aunt Maria's was the cause of all the trouble that happened to us, and a pretty muddle it was.

We went on up to the top, and there we met a delicious breeze, as cool as could be, and saw the view, — only there was so much of it that, of course, we couldn't half see it.

Hal said he wished he had eyes like telescopes, and Aunt Maria said she would be a fairy god-mother for once, and gratify his wish. Then she smiled and said: "Presto — change!" and pulled a big spy-glass out of the basket. We took turns looking through it. It was funny to see Baby Bunting; he always shut up the wrong eye.

By and by we had luncheon, and when we were rested we started down. After a while Aunt Maria and Susie wanted to sit down. Bo's'n said he "guessed he'd keep right on, and have the carriage ready for us when we got down." So off he went, with Baby Bunting on his shoulder.

Susie became so tired that Aunt Maria had to stop pretty often for her to rest, so Hal and I ran ahead. When we came to the place where the spring was, we remembered what Aunt Maria had said, so we struck into the woods to go over there, thinking she would stop when they came along.

Hal and I took a drink, and then went to work building a little dam, expecting every minute to hear Aunt Maria. We waited ever so long and didn't hear her, and so we filled our pail and came out upon the path. Aunt and Susie weren't there, and so we sat down and waited another long while; but still they didn't come. Then we thought perhaps they had gone past, and we hurried on.

After we'd gone about half a mile, we found in the path a whistle that I had made for Susie; then we knew they must be ahead, and ran as fast as we could to catch them.

Pretty soon we came to a place where the path branched off in two directions, which we hadn't noticed in going up. Hal and I took the left-hand path, which turned out to be the right one. We hurried down to the hotel, and there were Bo's'n and Baby sitting in the carriage; but they hadn't seen a sign of Aunt Maria. Then we knew right off that they must have taken the wrong path and gone astray.

We did n't wait a minute, but just turned round and cut right back. It was a pretty good distance, but it did n't take us long. It 's funny that we did n't think of taking Tearer, but we did n't; we left him behind in the carriage. We ran along the right-hand path, calling and whistling as loudly as we could, until pretty soon the path branched off again. Then we did n't know what to do. At last we agreed that Hal should go one way, and I the other, and come back to that spot to meet.

And now the muddle begins: Aunt Maria and Susie came out upon some road at the foot of the mountain, where they met a farmer driving along in an old-fashioned wagon, and he told them they were several miles away from the hotel, so they hired him to drive them around.

But meantime, Bo's'n thought something must have happened to us, and so he tied the horse and left Baby Bunting in the carriage, with Tearer to watch him, and he started off up the mountain to find us.

Then Baby Bunting got lonesome without any of us, and he got out of the carriage and went wandering about crying, until a lady found him and took him up to her room at the hotel; but all he could tell was that his name was Baby Bunting, and he lived on "The Extra Train," — which was n't very clear to the lady.

Then Aunt Maria drove up and found the empty

carriage, and was dreadfully frightened. She asked if anybody had seen a small child and a man and two boys. Nobody had seen the two boys and the child, but a man told her that he had seen Bo's'n get out of the carriage and start off up the mountain a few minutes before. Then Aunt Maria hired the man to go with her, and she started off up the mountain again.

Now to come back to myself: After I had followed my path a long way, and found it end in a swamp, I went back to wait for Hal at the spot appointed.

He didn't come; but while I was waiting, Bo's'n came up and found me. We stuck a note into the tree for Hal and started back. We met Aunt Maria and the man. Then Aunt Maria and I went back toward the carriage, and sent Bo's'n and the man to find Hal.

After Bo's'n had told Aunt Maria that he had left Baby Bunting in the carriage alone, you can imagine she didn't think of anything but finding the baby. We ran 'most all the way back. And then, lo and behold! Susy was gone too! Aunt Maria had left her in the carriage and charged her not to stir.

It seemed as if everybody was bewitched.

I thought Aunt Maria would faint away, she was so tired and excited. But it turned out all right: somebody had told Susie that her little brother was in the hotel, and she had gone in to see; and while Aunt Maria stood there so bewildered, they both came out on the piazza, and how they *did* run when they saw her!

Then I wanted to go off after Bo's'n and Hal, but Aunt Maria would n't let me. She said she had had Box-and-Cox enough. So we got into the carriage and waited; and pretty soon up came Hal from just the opposite direction that we expected, and after a long time poor Bo's'n came back with Tearer; and how he did grin when he saw us all seated in the carriage!

It was long after dark when we got back to "The Extra Train," and found the two servant-girls scared half to death at being left alone. And what do you think they said? Why, that Uncle Joe had come home and got alarmed about us, and he had started off toward the mountain to find us. Aunt Maria dropped into a chair and gasped out, —

"Oh, dear, this caps the climax!"

Bo's'n stood there looking dreadfully sorry for a minute; then all at once he brightened up and said:

"I 've got it! I 'll fetch him; never you fear, marm!"

Then he ran out to the stable. Hal and I wondered what he was going to do; but we were so tired we did n't follow.

In a minute there was a tremendous rushing noise outside, and we ran to the window and saw what it was.

Bo's'n had set off a sky-rocket!

We had a half-dozen left from the "Fourth," and Bo's'n set off three, one after another. Sure enough, it did the business! Uncle Joe saw them, and knew we must have got home, and that the signal was meant for him; so he came hurrying back, just in time to eat supper with us.

Aunt Maria said it seemed as if she was never so glad in her life, and that she had had enough of climbing mountains; that mountains were made to look at, but not to climb.

CHAPTER IV.

THE CANADIANS.

THE days went by, and we had lived a good while without anybody having come near us, so we never thought of there being any danger. We had no neighbors, you know, and folks could n't see us from the road. We were so hidden among the trees that they never suspected any one was living there. We used to play all around where we liked, and Aunt Maria used to go away to spend the day whenever she wanted, without worrying about us.

But at last we had our eyes opened. We had a

visit that we didn't forget. Hal and I used to
read Walter Scott's novels, and wished there were
castles nowadays, and we could be in one just
once, when it was besieged. We never thought
our wishes would be granted. But they were;
and this is the way it happened: —

One fine day, just after dinner, Aunt Maria took
Susie and started off for a town seven or eight
miles away, to do some shopping. Bo's'n went
with them to drive. The two servant girls had
done up their work and gone off for a walk in the
woods. Hal and I were out in the field. I was
painting the hull of a little ship we had been making for Baby Bunting, and Hal was fixing the rig-
ging in a way that Bo's'n had showed him. Baby
was inside, taking his afternoon nap on the parlor
sofa, and Tearer was lying on the floor by his
side.

It was just as still as it could be. The birds
had stopped singing because it was so warm, and
there wasn't any noise except the rustling of the
trees, and now and then a squirrel whistling in the
woods.

All at once Hal started up and said, —

" What 's that ? "

We listened, and heard a furious crackling of
dead branches in the woods, as if some one was
running, and in a minute more out rushed our
two girls, with their faces as white as a sheet.
Hal and I sprang up and asked what was the

matter. They could scarcely speak at first, but they managed to stammer out, —

"Ugh, ugh! Run, Mister Hal! Run, both o' yees!"

"What is it?"

"Oh, they're comin'! They'll kill us; they'll murther us, and ate us!"

"Who?"

"Thim wild Injuns; the woods is full of 'em! Quick! quick! Get into the kairs, like foine byes now; they won't lave a stitch of flesh on yer bones av they onct lay hands on yees!"

Hal and I began to laugh at this wild story; but just then there was a sound of trampling in the woods coming toward us, and we scrambled into the cars. Hal darted into the kitchen after the girls, and I was going to follow, but I happened to think of Baby Bunting, and rushed into the parlor-car.

Luckily, the two cars were well locked. The girls always locked up the dining-room between meals on account of the silver; and Aunt Maria had locked "the sleeper" before she went.

As soon as I had got in and locked both doors of the car, I stuck my head out of the window to see what it was. But I popped it in again as quick as a flash; for there, close to us, was a party of rough-looking men coming through the trees. Then I ran and pulled down all the blinds, so that they couldn't see into the car.

They came up and stared and stared all round "The Extra Train;" they could n't make it out. I could see them as plain as could be through the shutters. They were about as dark as Indians, but they were n't Indians. I did n't know what they were until I thought all at once of what Bo's'n had said about there being a party of Canadians encamped somewhere about the lake. I knew then it must be they.

They were rough, loaferish men, and I did n't like the looks of them at all. I wished I were in the same car with Hal. I wondered what he was doing. All the time, though, I kept a sharp watch on the Canadians. There were three middle-aged men and one young man.

Pretty soon they came up the steps and tried the door. Tearer jumped up; I grabbed him and stuffed my cap in his mouth to keep him from barking. But he is n't a barking dog, he does n't usually waste breath in barking; but when there's any danger he takes right hold. And so when I saw him get up and go to the door and stand there so still, with the shaggy hair bristling up all over his neck, I did n't feel quite so scared.

The Canadians tried hard to get in. They shook the door, they dashed against it, and they tried their best; but it was too strong for them. Then they went around and clambered up to look through the windows; but the blinds were shut, so they could n't see anything. I kept whispering to Tearer all the time, to keep him from growling. I thought perhaps if they did n't hear nor see anybody they might go away.

All at once the fellow at the window up with his fist and hit the pane a rousing crack. It was very thick glass and it did n't break; but I knew it would n't stand many such knocks as that. Just as he lifted up his fist to strike again, and I began to wonder what I should do, there was the sound of a gun, and the man jumped down to the ground like lightning.

I knew in a minute it was Hal, and I wanted to hurrah and clap my hands. He had opened the window and fired his shot-gun. I guess the Canadians were well scared, for they ran up to my end of the train, all four of them, and stood there under my windows, jabbering a lot of gibberish and looking around with an ugly scowl.

Just then I happened to see our little brass cannon under a chair in the corner. I knew it was loaded, — we always kept it loaded, but only with powder, of course, so as to be ready for a salute.

I picked it up, put it on a little table close to one of the windows, raised the sash softly, and *bang !* it went, right over their heads!

I thought they would all jump out of their skins! I giggled right out, but they did n't hear me; they ran as tight as they could go across the field, over by the stable, and hid in the bushes.

The cannon waked Baby Bunting, and he began to cry. I had to quiet him, and by that time the Canadians had rallied, and began to throw big stones to break the glass.

Crash! crash! went two of the windows in a twinkling. I began to be afraid again.

I saw two of them go creeping off through the woods, and I knew they meant some mischief. I was afraid they meant to set fire to the train.

Hal shot off his gun again, but I had no more powder.

The Canadians kept well behind the trees, — which showed they were afraid; but now and then one threw a stone. Luckily they were a good way off.

At last, when I was just beginning to hope they had got tired and gone away, I heard a queer little noise under the train. In a minute more we began to move. Then I knew what they had done: they had taken the blocks away from the wheels and pushed until they had set the car in motion. I was awfully scared at this; for it was a down grade clear to the main track, and if the train once got going I knew we could never stop it. Besides, it was 'most time for the regular express up-train, which would surely run into us and smash us all to atoms.

That made me really desperate. I didn't wait another instant, but opened the door and sprang out on the platform, yelling like a Mohawk. Hal came out of his car the same minute. I set Tearer on the Canadians, and we both sprang to the brakes.

As soon as we had stopped the train we looked back, and there were two of the Canadians running across the field, with Tearer at their heels. They disappeared in the woods. Hal loaded his gun with some more powder, and we went across toward the stable.

Somehow, we were n't so afraid now we had seen them run.

We heard a tremendous tussle going on in the woods. We hurried up, and when we got into the edge of the woods we found that Tearer had put the whole of them to flight!

He had seized one by the coat-tail, and the fellow just slipped out of the coat and ran for his life.

Then Tearer pulled another down, and was just going to spring upon him, when another Canadian came up with a big club and cracked Tearer over the head.

Then Tearer turned upon him, and the first one got up and ran like a deer. The fellow with the club fought like a tiger for a few mnutes; but at last he dropped his stick and darted up a tree.

Tearer flew after him, growling furiously; but the Canadian managed to draw himself up to a big limb out of the way. Then Tearer sat down at the foot of that tree and held him prisoner.

"TEARER WAS STILL KEEPING THE MAN PRISONER IN THE TREE."

The fellow shouted to us, and talked a lot of gibberish, but we could n't understand him. We went up and patted Tearer on the head and pointed to the man, and told him not to let his prisoner escape, and we knew he would n't.

When we got back to the train, there was the carriage, and there was Aunt Maria hugging Baby Bunting and listening to the story which the two girls were telling of the "wild Injuns."

Hal and I made believe 't was n't much of anything, so as not to scare Aunt Maria; but we told Bo's'n about the man in the tree, and he slipped out there to look at him, as soon as he had put up the horse. He patted Tearer, and nodded his head, and muttered, —

"We 've got *you* trapped, my fine feller!"

We expected Uncle Joe early that afternoon, and he came just at sundown. We took him out to the barn and told him all about the whole affair, and how the tramp was "treed."

Uncle Joe flared up like gunpowder. He said things had come to a pretty pass if folks could n't be safe from savages in New England, by this time. He said he would send those fellows packing that very night, and told Bo's'n to harness up the horse right away.

Then he went out into the woods where Tearer was still keeping the man prisoner in the tree. Uncle Joe called the dog off, and told the man to come down.

At first the man was n't going to; but Uncle Joe
has an air of authority about him. He is used to
commanding men, and he put on a stern look
which the man did n't dare disobey. So at last
he came sneaking down, and Uncle Joe marched
him back to the stable, and made him get into
the wagon. Then Uncle Joe got in, took the
reins, and drove away.

It was about an hour before dark. They drove
a couple of miles over to where one of the select-
men of the town lived.

Uncle Joe got him, and then they went and
hunted up the Canadians in their camp down by
the lake, made them pack up their duds in their
old tumble-down wagons, and clear off out of the
town. Uncle Joe and the selectman followed them
for several miles, and threatened to arrest them if
they were ever seen in those parts again.

And now my story draws to a close. There are
a great many things more I should like to tell, but
I guess you must be tired by this time. The summer was 'most gone, and there were only a few
more days left of vacation; but I must tell you
about the end of it, for that was real funny, — the
funniest of the whole, I think, and makes it all
seem now, to look back upon, almost like a fairy
story.

We had had a splendid time. We were awfully
sorry to go home; we knew, of course, we should

have to go pretty soon, but we did n't ask any questions, — we did n't like to think about it. Uncle Joe and Aunt Maria had n't said anything either; but at last, one evening, — it was Friday night, I remember, — Uncle Joe went out to the door about nine o'clock, and came back pretty soon, saying he guessed it was going to rain, and we 'd better get our playthings in.

We were in the midst of a game of "Logomachy," round the parlor table; but we jumped up and went out, and got in all our traps. It was real cloudy, and we thought Uncle Joe was right about the rain, and never suspected anything, but went to bed as innocent as lambs.

But were n't we astonished in the morning, though ! I waked up pretty early; I had been having dreams of rolling off a precipice and flying through the air, and lots of disagreeable things. I went to the window and looked out, rubbed my eyes, looked again, turned around and stared at Hal, rubbed my head, looked again, and finally roared out to Hal to get up and see what under the sun was the matter. He came to the window and rubbed *his* eyes.

What do you suppose it was ? Why, the lake was gone, the mountain had disappeared, and there we were standing in the midst of a strange town. Finally, Aunt Maria came in laughing, and told us we were half way home; that Uncle Joe had ordered a locomotive to come up on pur-

pose to take us; that we had started very early, so
as not to interfere with the regular trains; that
we were "watering up" now, and should go on in
a minute; and, finally, that it was time for us to
get up, for breakfast was almost ready.

We hurried, and were ready in less than no time.
It seemed queer enough to be sitting there, the
whole family about the breakfast-table, as comfortable as could be, while the cars were flying
along like the wind.

When we arrived at our own station and got up
to go, it almost seemed like leaving home. We
all felt rather down in the mouth, I guess; but
just as we alighted on the platform, something
happened that made us all laugh.

A man with a big carpet-bag, bundle, and umbrella came rushing up to Uncle Joe, all out of
breath, and asked: "What train is this?"

"This," said Uncle Joe, with a twinkle in his
eye, "this, sir, is 'The Extra Train.'"

IV.

THE DISCONTENTED DOWAGER.

6

IV.

THE DISCONTENTED DOWAGER.

ONCE upon a time, in the drawing-room of a
stately mansion, there hung a very fine portrait all framed in a golden frame, and swung from
the cornice by a thick silken cord. This portrait,
which had been painted long ago by a famous
artist, was the picture of an old dowager, —
which means, you know, a grand old lady, — with
very red cheeks, very bright eyes, very thick gray
hair, and very fat neck and arms. She was
dressed in a red velvet gown, with the funniest
short waist you ever saw in your lives; she wore a
splendid necklace about her throat, bracelets upon
both arms, and ever so many rings on her fingers,
while her hair was twisted up into a queer-looking
bunch on the top of her head, and trimmed with
ribbons and rich ostrich-plumes. It was evident
the old dowager must have been a high and mighty
person while she lived, not only from this fine
attire, but from a very commanding look in her
sharp eyes and a very proud expression about her
firm lips.

But it was years and years since the old dowager
had lived, and a great many changes had taken

place in the world. People did n't go around in short waists and ostrich plumes any longer, and did n't do a good many other things it was thought right and proper to do in the old dowager's time; and so as she looked down from the wall and saw what folks did and how they lived nowadays, she was very much astonished, and also — though she ought not to have been — very much disgusted. Indeed, if the family that lived in the house could have heard the old dowager's remarks upon them when they had gone to bed and the lights were put out, — remarks addressed to the other portraits in the room, and especially to a fat, puffy-looking old gentleman in a wig and ruffled shirt, who hung opposite, — 1 am afraid their feelings would have been hurt very much. It was then the old dowager used to open those tight red lips, and wink those bright gray eyes, and speak her mind freely about the things she saw and heard to the puffy old gentleman, who thus was robbed of his rest to such an extent that it was no wonder he always looked sleepy and stupid.

In short, the old dowager found so many things to scold about, and so many new aggravations occurred every day, that soon she spent the whole of every night in railing, and gave the other portraits no peace of their lives. She never stopped to think how much better off she was than a portrait on the other side of the room, of a bare-legged boy with a dirty face, painted by a Mr.

Murillo, or another portrait close by her side, painted by a Mr. Raphael, of a certain Saint Cecilia who not only had no ostrich plume to her head, but not even a shoe or stocking to her foot!

Do you want to know what were the things the dowager complained of? Why, there were so many I cannot remember half of them. She complained of the impudent way in which people came up and stared at her, and made remarks about her clothes and person; but then she complained even more when they went past and took no notice of her. She scolded now because there was too much light in the room, so that her fine points could not be seen; again, because there was n't light enough. She scolded because the housemaids dusted her face with a brush, as though she had been a chair or a table; but she scolded twice as hard if she were not dusted. She would fly into the most dreadful passion if any one dared to talk too loudly in the room, and yet she fell into a rage of curiosity and jealousy if they spoke in a whisper or withdrew out of ear-shot. Then the flies lit on her face, and bit her and tickled her nose, so that — as she told the old gentleman — she felt a constant inclination to sneeze, which spoiled her expression. But worse than all, spiders — ugh-h! black, long-legged spiders! — got behind her frame and crawled up her back; "and she just wanted the family to understand she could n't and would n't bear it, and some day she would scream out and

tear her canvas." Again, the family used to go
to bed nights and let the fires out, and the house
became so chilled that she told the old gentleman
she was sure she should catch her death o' cold
and go into a decline. "Why," she exclaimed,
savagely, "*they* crawl into their warm beds and
tuck themselves in, but they seem to think *I* am
made of cast iron!"

But her greatest grievance was the children,
who sometimes came to play in the room where
she was hung. There were only two, to be sure,
— a little boy and a little girl, — but the dowager
did n't approve of their presence, and so she
watched them with jealous eyes to see that they
did no mischief, though I grieve to say they sometimes did. At first they never thought of the old
dowager's watching them, till one day the little
girl took down her mother's beautiful portfolio,
— which she had been forbidden to touch, — and
was strewing the pictures all over the floor, when
she happened to look up, and caught the dowager's
eye fixed sternly upon her. And what do you
think she did? Tremble and run away? No; I am
shocked to say she made a grimace. Think of
making a face at your great-great-great-grand-
mother! How do you suppose she dared to do it?
But that was nothing to what the little boy did;
for once when he was playing with his rubber ball
in the parlor, which he had been expressly forbidden to do, the old dowager frowned on him so

sternly that he threw the rubber ball, — the saucy
little wretch, — and struck his g-g-g-grandmother
in the eye! I really do not know what might
have happened then, — very likely the old dowager
would have come straight down from the wall and
punished him on the spot, — if his mother had not
come in.

This was the last time the children ever troubled
her, for thenceforth they were kept out of the room;
but, none the less, the old dowager fell into such
an intolerable habit of carping and fault-finding
that she made not only herself miserable, but all
the other portraits as well; and though she found
only food for ridicule and censure in the sayings
and doings of the people about her, she nevertheless spent her whole time in listening to and
watching them, instead of improving her mind by
reading the book in her lap, into which she was
never seen to look.

At length, misfortune fell upon the family to
which the old dowager belonged, and their stately
mansion, the furniture, and all their valuables
were sold at auction. A rude and curious crowd
thronged the rooms, and poked canes and umbrellas at the old dowager, and laughed at her
bracelets and ostrich plumes, and made jokes about
her. Then she and the puffy old gentleman were
put up for sale, and knocked down at a very low
price to a dirty, hook-nosed man, who carted them
away to a dark, dingy shop; and there he took the

old dowager out of her fine frame and put another picture in it, and sold it; and after a few days he packed the poor crest-fallen old lady away in a dark, musty loft, where a lot of rubbish was piled upon her, squeezing her dreadfully. There she lay year after year, while the dust gathered thick upon her, and the spiders made their webs all about her, and the mice ran over her face, and the moths gnawed great holes in her fine velvet gown, till at last, when after a long time she was taken down, she was such a sorry-looking object that she was ruthlessly torn into strips and thrown into the ash-barrel.

V.

HERCULES–JACK.

V.

HERCULES-JACK.

NOT his real name, of course not. His father and mother would never have given him such a name as that. His real name was John Franklin Holmes, and there was n't a wooden bench, a gate-post, or barn-door within a mile of his father's house on which the initials "J. F. H." might not have been found, cut by a very busy but somewhat battered jack-knife.

Hercules-Jack was only a nickname he had picked up, and you shall judge how fairly he came by it when I have told you a little more about him.

Johnny, or Jack, Holmes, as he was oftener called, was just ten years old. Jack was round and chubby, with red hair, blue eyes, and a freckled nose that turned up the least bit in the world at the end.

Did I say he was plump? If I did n't I should do so at once, for that was the very first thing that struck you about Jack: he was very plump, — indeed, I may say extremely plump; his cheeks were as round as apples, there were dimples in the backs of his hands, and his jacket fitted him as tightly as a skin does a sausage.

Now this was a sore point with Jack, especially as the boys used to laugh at him sometimes because he was so fat; but perhaps Jack would not have minded the boys very much if one day he had not overheard Polly Joy whisper to Susie Ditson, when he was standing behind their desk doing a sum in vulgar fractions upon the blackboard, that he was "a ridiculous little dumpling." This was too much; it shot a pang into poor Jack's heart.

For, to whisper to you a secret, Jack very much admired Polly. He thought her cheeks were the rosiest, her braids were the longest, her dresses were the finest, her hats the prettiest, and that she herself was altogether the nicest girl in the big round world.

Poor Jack! Polly's unkind remark rankled in his bosom. After brooding over it for several days, he awoke one morning and took a sudden resolution. He clenched his teeth, pounded his fat little fist on the table, and exclaimed,—

"If I am a dumpling, I'll do something that all the thin boys in the world couldn't do."

Jack's round little head was full of schemes, his throbbing little heart was full of courage; he had a spirit big enough for a giant, while his ambition, for a ten-year-old boy, was really quite tremendous.

Now Jack had read a good many books of adventure; there was nothing he liked better than to pore over the doings of knights and dwarfs, giants, dragons, and magicians, and that sort of people. Especially he admired and reverenced Jack the Giant Killer, while he bemoaned that there were no giants left for him to destroy.

He thought of other ways of distinguishing himself. He considered the merits of highwaymen and pirates; but as he knew that people in these professions nearly always came to bad ends, and as there was no lonely road where he could wait for travellers, and no fleet horse to ride, and as no convenient ocean lay near his father's house, and there was no way of his getting a long, low, black schooner, if the ocean had been there, he gave up these plans.

Finding these roads to distinction shut to him, Jack went about for a while quite dejected, until one day he came across an old book of mythology in the library, and there read of the exploits of Hercules, the great hero of antiquity, who performed twelve celebrated "labors," or heroic deeds. Jack's eyes glowed as he read the wonderful narrative. Again and again he pored over the record with bated breath and kindled imagination. And as he read of the mighty deeds of this great hero, a purpose gradually took root in his mind. *He* would be another such hero, — a modern Hercules. The thought thrilled him. He brooded over it by day; it haunted his dreams by night. He went about with a lofty look on his face. He already regarded the other boys with the pity and compassion with which a real hero would perhaps regard common men.

But how to become a Hercules, — that was the next question. There were no roaring lions, no savage wild boars, no many-headed hydras in the little village where he lived. Neither did centaurs abound; indeed, Jack had never seen one in his life; "but then," he thought to himself, "there must be plenty of other terrible and wonderful things to do," and so his resolution was taken.

But how to begin ?

"I 've got to do something first to get up a name before I begin on the 'labors,'" said Jack. "Hercules strangled the snakes, — I 'm rather afraid of snakes. But stop! the first thing to do is to get a club; of course that 's the main thing. With the right sort of a club, the 'labors' themselves can't amount to very much."

Accordingly, Jack spent days traversing the woods with an old axe, in search of a club. After a long hunt, he at length decided upon a hickory sapling with a formidable knot, about four feet from the ground, which could be cut so as to bring this knot at the end of the club. With patient toil Jack cut down, trimmed, and peeled and whittled and polished this hickory stick, which when done was fully as long as himself; and indeed he could only wield it by using both hands and putting forth all his strength.

Now, at length, he was ready to begin. He drew a long breath. What should he do? He pondered the question long and anxiously. It was very strange, but now when he came to look about him, there really was nothing wonderful to do. Life was surprisingly peaceful and humdrum, and pitifully tame. The most discouraging thing was the lack of ferocious monsters. There was an utter dearth of monsters. Jack couldn't understand why these interesting creatures only abounded in ancient times.

One day, while Jack was still puzzling over the question of what he should do first, one of the neighbors came into the house and began to tell about her little boy who had just barely escaped being tossed by old Sol Stevens's bull.

Here was an opportunity. This was what Jack was waiting for, and he immediately decided upon a plan of action.

Sol Stevens was a crabbed man who lived down a long lane, and owned an old bull as crabbed as himself. Again and again the boys and girls, and indeed grown-up women and men, had been chased and scared by this savage beast, who, not content with his own domain, had a vicious habit of leaping fences and roaming about the highway. Many complaints had been made to old Sol without avail, and the bull had become the terror of the neighborhood. It was almost strange Jack had not thought of him before.

He now at once determined upon an encounter with the bull. But first he went down the lane and took a private look at the creature from behind a stone wall. He seemed so little formidable as he stood peacefully grazing in the meadow that Jack promised himself an easy task in his subjugation.

In playing the part of Hercules, it was desirable, of course, to look as much like that hero as possible; accordingly, one fine afternoon Jack slipped off to the barn with a big bundle under his arm, and there proceeded to dress himself as nearly as he could like the picture in the old mythology.

As Hercules had bare legs and arms in the picture, Jack first tucked up his own trousers and sleeves and tied them securely to his waist and shoulders; then for the lion's skin, which the hero wore, Jack fastened about his shoulders a bright red sheepskin mat which he borrowed from the hall in the house. Next throwing off his hat, tossing his hair about as much like the picture as possible, Jack seized his club and strode up and down the barn floor, feeling so brave and confident that it may be doubted if Hercules himself ever felt more so.

Thus equipped, Jack at length marched off down the lane, accompanied by three or four of his comrades whom he had let into the secret. Precisely what he was going to do, or how he was

going to do it, he evidently had no clear notion; but
in this he was only like a great many other heroes
after all. However, the first thing was, of course,
to seek his prey. On and on he went down the
lane, his bare legs blue with the cold, the sheepskin flapping up and down on his back, and the big
club — too heavy to carry — dragged along behind.

Arrived at the bottom of the lane, the boys stationed themselves upon the wall, while Jack
jumped over into the pasture where the bull was.
He did n't walk quite so proudly and erect here
as in the lane; he took shorter steps, — there was,
perhaps, less occasion for striding now that he
was near at hand. However, he advanced slowly
and cautiously toward the distant herd of cattle.
Now and then he turned around in a deliberative
way. His pace grew steadily slower. At length,
when he was still some yards distant, the bull
unexpectedly lifted his head to brush away a fly,
and brought Jack to a sudden standstill. Reflect-
ing, however, that Hercules would probably not
have acted in this way, Jack plucked up courage
and marched boldly up very near to the unsuspect-
ing bull. Jack had read somewhere that the most
wild and savage beast cannot endure the gaze of
the human eye, and he therefore resolved to over-
awe the bull first with his eye, and then complete
his subjugation at his leisure.

With this intent he planted himself about a
yard distant from the bull, and putting his arm

akimbo, glared fiercely at him. The unconscious animal peacefully continued his grazing. No doubt, if he could have known who Jack was, and what was his errand, or if he had understood that when a small boy goes about bareheaded with his trousers tucked up and the parlor mat tied to his back, that means Hercules, and that Hercules was a hero, and that Jack meant to be another hero, and had now fixed his small blue eyes upon him with the intent of striking terror to his heart, — no doubt, I say, if the bull could have understood all this, he would have been terribly frightened, and would have shaken in every limb; and par- . ticularly, if he had only cast his eye upon that club, and understood it was intended for him, I am sure he would have run away as fast as his legs could carry him. As it was, the stupid creature did nothing of the sort; he kept on quietly grazing, and paying no more attention to Jack than if he had been a post.

This was too humiliating for a hero to endure. The boys from the top of the distant wall already began to shout derisively, —

"Don't be afraid; give it to him! Punch him in the ribs! Stare him out of countenance! Knock his horns off! Twist his tail!"

Jack advanced a little nearer; he coughed, he flourished his club. Presently, incited by the cries of the boys, he picked up a stone and threw it at the passive animal.

The bull lifted his head, and for the first time looked attentively at Jack, who immediately struck an attitude and glared at him. To his astonishment, the bull did not quail in the least; on the contrary, as if suddenly appreciating Jack's hostile purpose, he glared back so angrily and fiercely that Jack became very much discomfited, and began slowly to retire. The bull tossed his head, uttered a low bellow, and stood watching Jack attentively. The red mat, about this time, began to slip from Jack's shoulder, and he pulled it up so that it hung in front of him, when at once, as if maddened by the sight, the bull made a furious rush at his antagonist. Jack did not wait to try the effect of the human eye any longer, — indeed, he forgot all about the human eye, he forgot all about Hercules and every other hero, ancient or modern; but throwing his club at the rushing animal, he fled to a small apple-tree, which fortunately was near at hand. The bull stopped to toss the club, and this gave Jack a minute's time, and saved his life; for he had only just scrambled up to the nearest branch when the vicious beast came bellowing up underneath. Jack was now a prisoner, and was just making up his mind that he would have to spend a long time in the tree, when the boys suddenly set up a great shout of, —

"Look out, Jack; old Sol's coming!"

And, sure enough, old Sol was coming; there he was, letting down the bars now to take his cattle

home. Jack kept very still, and hoped he would
not be discovered, for he was even more afraid of
old Sol than of the bull.

But the unfortunate red mat caught old Sol's
eye, and he came marching across to see what was
that red thing in his tree.

"Come down here, you young rascal! What are
you doing up my apple-tree?" he cried, as he
recognized Jack.

"Nothin', sir; the bull chased me!"

"Well, what business had you in this field
where the bull could get at you? You came to
steal my apples; I know you!"

"Oh, I d-did n't, sir! no, indeed I d-did n't!"

"Come down here, I tell ye. What are you
doin' with that door-mat on your back, eh?"

"Oh, please," cried Jack, his teeth chattering
with fear, "I was only playing Hercules!"

"I 'll 'Hercules' ye!" cried old Sol, seizing
Jack as he came down the tree and shaking him
roughly. "Let me ever ketch ye in my apple-tree
ag'in, and I 'll — ye miserable young urchin!"

Here now was hero Jack in the strong grasp of
an angry man, and with a stick in the air ready
to come down on his back.

Then arose such indignant and significant shouts
from the group of boys on the wall that Sol Stevens
turned. Jack saw his chance and made a sudden
spring. His collar tore off in the old man's hand,
and the culprit was soon safely over the wall, and

making the best of his way home, surrounded by the boys, who were waiting in the lane, and who by turns ridiculed him and congratulated him on his escape.

Jack would n't have minded the boys; but just as he turned out of the lane upon the road, whom should he see coming along but Susie Ditson and Polly Joy.

The more Jack tried to hide, the more the boys would n't let him. There was a pretty lively scramble. The girls heard, looked up, and saw a squirming mass of dark coats and trousers pushing forward a red-faced boy, whose plump arms were waving wildly, while a woolly red door-mat dangled about his bare legs.

Then came a halt, a sudden wrench, and away flew Jack down the road, even faster than he had fled from the bull. And this was the last that was seen in public of John Franklin Holmes in the character of Hercules.

VI.

OUR SPECIAL ARTIST.

VI.

OUR SPECIAL ARTIST.

NOW, boys and girls, this is going to be a
true story, — at least mostly true; and true
stories, you know (or, if you don't know, some day
or other you will find out), are often a good deal
stranger and funnier than made-up ones. Not
that this story is going to be very, very strange,
or very, very funny; but it will be strange and
funny enough, I hope, to be interesting, — at any
rate, it is just what might happen to any boy who
should go and do what Ben Brady did. But perhaps I should begin by telling who Ben Brady
was. Well, then, Ben Brady was, or rather *is*, —
for Ben is alive and well this very minute, — a
nice, bright boy who lives in the pretty country
town of Dashville, and is the only son of Mrs.
Elizabeth Brady, a widow, who regards Ben as the
apple of her eye. Ben is really fourteen years
old; but you would never in the world suspect it,
for he is n't a bit bigger than Johnny Townsend,
across the way, who will not be twelve till the
fifth day of next October. Now, it was just because

he was so small that everybody thought what Ben did was so wonderful. It really was n't so very extremely wonderful, as you will see, but it certainly was rather odd. In the first place, he went and bought a tourograph. What! you don't know what a tourograph is ? Why, my dears, it 's nothing in the world but a photographic apparatus to take pictures at home. Ben had saved up a little money which he had earned doing chores out of school, and when he heard what a fashionable thing it is nowadays for young gentlemen and ladies to take pictures at home, and when he found out how easily it is done, and that it does n't cost a great deal, he quietly made up his mind, and without saying anything to anybody he went off and bought a camera, and a three-legged standard to hold the camera, and the little frames to print with, and the ruby light, and a lot of dry plates, all prepared to take pictures on, and a little piece of black cloth to go over his head and shut out the light when he squinted into the camera, and in fact the whole apparatus, and took them home to his astonished mamma.

Next, he lost no time in turning his room into a photographic gallery, moved the bed and the chairs into a corner, put up some cotton screens, made a romantic landscape, representing a weeping willow, a broken pillar, and an urn, out of some strips of wall-paper, for his sitters to pose before; and having turned the whole room into a scene of

wild confusion, made spots all over the carpet, and
filled the air with a bad smell of chemicals, he
declared himself ready to take pictures. He began
practising upon his mamma, his aunt Hannah, his
cousin Jane, and the cook, filling in odd times
with the dog and cat when he could n't get people.
The fact that these early pictures were not a suc-
cess, and that only the most experienced eye could
distinguish his aunt Hannah from the cook, did
not in the least discourage Ben. He laid the
blame wholly upon the sitters themselves, declar-
ing that he never could make any of them " look
lively," or hold their chins high enough in the
air; although his cousin Jane indignantly declared
she held *her* chin just as high as it would go, and
as for looking lively, *she* was n't going to sit
ten minutes grinning at a crack in the wall
for anybody.

Perhaps by this time you have all found out that
Ben was a spoiled child. Well, I must confess
he was, if not exactly spoiled, at least very much
petted and indulged. His mother let him have
his own way in everything which was not really
wrong or harmful. So this was how it happened
that he was allowed to go away with the Dashville
cadets on their annual camping-out excursion.
Ben's cousin, William Jones, was a lieutenant in
the cadets, and he promised to take care of Ben if
his mother would let him go. Thereupon, Ben
began to tease his mother; and as he had always

been a pretty good boy and had never got into
serious mischief, and as she had great confidence
in Lieutenant Jones, and as, moreover, she knew it
would be a bitter disappointment to Ben if she
said no, she finally consented. Then you ought
to have seen Ben and heard Ben; he jumped over
the chairs and he shouted "Hurrah!" till he was
quite hoarse ; he ran over and got Johnny Townsend, and marched up and down all the rest of the
day, beating a drum, and made poor Johnny go
before, waving a flag till his little arms ached
again.

And so, for the next day and two or three days
afterward, — in fact, till it was time for them to
go, — there was nothing heard but "camping out."
In an unlucky moment Ben determined to take
his tourograph, and that is how I came to tell
this story; for if he had left the tourograph at
home I should have had no story to tell.

By and by the day came. Ben was up early and
packed his apparatus safely in the bottom of his
trunk, while his good-natured mamma put his
clothes all about it, so that it might not break; and
among other things she put in a nice box, contain-
ing paper and envelopes and postage-stamps and a
stylographic pen, and made Ben promise to write
her home a letter every other day, to let her know
he was safe and well.

Pretty soon the carriage came, and away they
whisked to the depot. And here there was a fine

bustle. All the boys in town were assembled, and a big crowd of grown-up people beside; the band was playing gayly, the cadets had just arrived, and were that moment wheeling up in front of the platform; a large flag was flying over the depot, and the people were cheering at the tops of their voices. Ben's heart bounded with delight. He felt himself so like a soldier going off to the wars, and such a very bold and martial spirit took possession of him, and he so longed to be a cadet and have a handsome blue-and-white uniform, and he was altogether so filled and inflated with enthusiasm that his very jacket-buttons nearly burst off.

"There he is!" cried Johnny Townsend from the midst of the crowd, pointing at Ben; whereupon all the other boys set up a great shout, and were as envious of Ben as Ben was of the cadets. Indeed, they could scarcely believe their eyes when they presently saw Lieutenant Jones go and help Ben out of the carriage, and then take him up and actually introduce him to the captain.

But pretty soon the steam-whistle began to toot, and the bell to ring, and the band to play again; and then the cadets filed into the cars, and their sweethearts handed them pretty bouquets through the windows, and everybody said good-by at least a half-dozen times; and so at last off they went, singing " Sherman's March Through Georgia."

It took them some hours to get to the place where they were going, so that it was nearly sun-

set when they arrived. The camping-ground was
a beautiful field, bounded on the north and east by
some dark green woods, and sloping on the west
toward the highway, commanding, too, a distant
view of the sea. Such a hubbub as there was un-
packing and getting to rights! Ben was delighted.
The men went straight to work pitching their tents
and making up their little cot-beds; the cooks
hurried to and fro, making fires and getting out
their pots and pans to cook supper; the guards
were mounted, and all were as busy as so many
bees.

Ben was assigned to Lieutenant Jones's quarters,
where, after a hearty supper, he went straight to
bed, quite tired out with all the fatigue and
excitement.   •

The next morning Ben was awakened early by
the réveille, or, as the cadets all called it, "the
revelay," and, springing up, dressed himself
hastily and hurried out to the field, which looked
as though it had been strewn with jewels, all glittering as it was in the morning dew. And there
were the cadets, already drawn up in their fatigue-
dress, going through the roll-call. The woods
behind resounded with the songs of birds, while
far off lay the dark-blue sea sparkling in the sun's
rays. Altogether, it was such a beautiful picture
that it straightway reminded Ben of his tourograph, and so he went directly and got out the
instrument.

Off to the left of the field there was a little green knoll, from which the camp looked very pretty, with the group of white tents pitched on the green grass, the colors floating from the flag-staff in the morning breeze, and the soldiers gathered in little knots here and there for conversation. Thither Ben went to set up his camera, and directly a group of soldiers gathered about him, wondering what such a little boy was doing with such a big instrument. Ben was at first somewhat abashed, and looked very sheepish to find himself the centre of such a group of spectators. They asked him a great many questions as he was adjusting his lens, and were very curious to see the result of his work. Ben had never taken any pictures out-of-doors before, and was anxious to see them himself. So, when he had taken three or four views, he hurried back to the tent to develop them, quite nervous with anticipation of the wonder and admiration his pictures would excite.

But I must stop here a minute to explain to all those girls and boys who don't know already just how to take a photograph, that there are two or three things necessary in order to make a picture. First, you have to put your plate into the camera, pull off the little cap in front, and expose it to the sunlight. You all know that part of it so well that I need not explain it. Now, ever so many people think that is all there is to be done, that the picture is now taken, and there's an end of

it. Well, so it is taken; but you would never
know it. The plate looks just exactly as it did
before you put it into the camera. There is n't
a sign of a picture on it, — not a line, not a
mark, *that you can see.* But — and this is the
wonder — the picture really is there all the time,
although you cannot see it. So the next thing
to do is to bring it out; that 's what is called
"developing" it. And how do you suppose they
do it ? Why, they take it into a very dark place,
and pour on it a kind of fluid with a difficult name,
and soak it in this fluid till pretty soon one little
point, then another little point, then the whole
outline, and at last the entire picture, grows
straight out of the plate like a ship coming through
a fog. It is a very strange and beautiful thing;
and I solemnly assure you that not all the fairies
and witches and magicians and enchanters, in all
your nursery-books put together, ever did anything half so wonderful and beautiful.

And now, what do you think ? Why, when Ben
hurried off to the tent, with all the soldiers following behind him, to develop his pictures, he
found he had forgotten to bring this mysterious
fluid with the hard name; and there he was, little
better off than if he had not taken his pictures, for
he could not show them. He threw his hat on
the bed, he stamped on the ground, he tried to
tear his hair in his vexation, only fortunately it
had been cut too short. But there was no help

for it; he had to come out and explain to the soldiers about the magic liquid, and he felt very silly and he looked very foolish, for he had fondly hoped to strike them dumb with astonishment.

However, if he could n't develop his pictures, he could at least *take* them, and keep them shut up from the light, and carry them home to develop. And so every day he went about, setting up his camera and disappearing under the mysterious black cloth, till he became a familiar object in the camp, and a group of the idle soldiers would usually gather about him whenever he appeared with his instrument.

Meantime, in the tents and at mess, he was introduced to all the officers, who thought it was so droll to see such a little boy making pictures that they took a good deal of notice of him. Indeed, they each and all sat to him for their pictures, from the sergeant up to the captain, who, leaning upon his sword, with his right hand thrust into his bosom, and his mustache brushed out into very fierce points, looked almost as grand as the late Louis Napoleon.

Ben was as proud as a peacock at being trusted to take all these pictures, and explained over and over again to every sitter that as soon as he got home he would develop them and send to each one proofs of his own photograph. Upon the strength of this promise every officer ordered a dozen or two to be struck off, and insisted upon paying for them in advance. Several of the common soldiers and the band did likewise; so that Ben soon became not only a distinguished personage in the camp, but collected such a sum of money that it quite turned his head. Straightway he began to look upon himself as an experienced artist and equal to anything. Indeed, he was called by the good-natured officers "Our Special Artist," and one of them printed these words upon a large ornamental badge which Ben wore tied around his cap.

As a result of all this prominence poor Ben became so puffed up with vanity that I very much doubt if a vainer little boy was ever heard of. You may easily see this for yourselves by the letters he wrote to his mamma. Here is one of them: —

CAMP BISMARCK.

DEAR MA, — I'm having royal good times. This is a jolly place. They have the best things to eat you ever saw. I wish you and Aunt Hannah could just taste the chowder. I have just as many plates of pudding as I want, and don't have any water in my coffee. I'm as fat as a pig. I've got so I can take photergrafs first rate. It's just as.easy as nothing now. I've taken 'most everybody's. I've got lots of orders too. I think I shall leave school when I come home and go into bisness, and then we can have a horse and buggy and a new parlor carpet. I have made up my mind to join the cadets this fall; the officers all like me 'most to death. They call me "Our Special Artist," and

Lieutenant Wilder made me a badge to wear with that printed on ; so you see that I put on as much style as anybody.

Oh! I forgot to tell you I came away without my developer, and so I can't finish a single plate. It was a horrid mistake, and I felt awful cut up at first; but I shall fetch home all my neggertives, and just go right at it and do it all up at once. You can tell Johnny Townsend that he need n't expect me to go fishing any more. I sha' n't have any time to go fooling round now with him. Please send me down two or three dozen more plates right away.

Your affectionate son,

BEN.

Meantime, Ben was taken about everywhere by the officers, and introduced to all the visitors at the camp as "Our Special Artist," to whom, with a great air, he always made the military salute, putting his heels close together, sticking out his forefinger, and touching the visor of his cap with a motion as stiff as a poker.

But the proudest and happiest day Ben had ever yet known was when the Governor and his staff came down to review the troops. Ben was duly marched up and introduced to his Excellency, who patted him on the head and called him "my little man," and said he should esteem it a great honor to sit to him for a picture. The Governor, of course, was merely joking, and only wanted to pay Ben a compliment. But the latter had become by this time so confident of his ability and so proud of his reputation that he took the Governor at his word; and accordingly, at dress parade in the afternoon, when his Excellency was standing watching the manœuvres of the troops, surrounded by his staff in their brilliant uniforms, with plumes flying and golden epaulets gleaming in the sunshine, Ben, nothing abashed, marched boldly forth, and setting up his instrument at a short distance, levelled it full at the distinguished party, and began adjusting the lens. Pretty soon some one pointed him out to the Governor, who was very much amused, and was good-natured enough to send a member of his staff, with his sword clanking and his black horse prancing, across to Ben, requesting him to shake a handkerchief when he was ready, and they would all stand quietly to be taken. Ben did as he was asked, and triumphantly took the picture in the face and eyes of the whole corps and a multitude of spectators gathered to witness the review.

Afterward, when the Governor was riding from the field, he suddenly drew up at sight of Ben and his instrument, and, stooping from his horse, said, —

"Good-by, my little artist; I shall expect one of those pictures when they are done!"

Ben, rigid as a lightning-rod, gave the military salute, and almost broke his forefinger by striking it so energetically against his visor.

BEN TAKING THE GOVERNOR.

This event was, indeed, the crowning feather in Ben's cap thus far. His cousin, Lieutenant Jones, laughed, and said, "He has grown six inches taller already, and pretty soon we shall have to get a ladder to climb up to him."

That same evening, as it chanced, several of the officers were gathered in one of the tents, where each in turn told some strange experiences that had happened to himself or his friends. Among others, Lieutenant Wilder related several thrilling adventures he had met with in Virginia amid the wild and beautiful scenery of the Shenandoah region, where he had lived for a time.

"Yes," he said, concluding, and at the same time patting Ben upon the head, "if I had only had 'Our Special Artist' there with me, I could have shown you some of the scenes where these things happened, and there's nothing like them in the country."

Ben was so grateful for this tribute in his honor that he asked many questions about Virginia, which led Lieutenant Wilder to go on and tell other stories of the lovely scenery of that State and the pleasant people he had met there, to all of which Ben listened with most attentive ears.

But the secret of this sudden interest in Virginia was explained at the end of the week, when the camp broke up. When everything was packed and sent off, and everybody was ready to march to the depot, "Our Special Artist" could not be found.

Search was made for him high and low, up in the
woods, down by the sea-shore, but all in vain; till
at length, just as everybody was becoming very
much alarmed, a little boy came up and handed
a note to Lieutenant Jones. He opened it quickly,
and read as follows : —

DEAR COUSIN BILL, — I guess your eyes will stick
out when you get this. I've gone to Virginia. I was
going to speak to you at first, but then I thought you'd
make a fuss, and so I thought I wouldn't. I'm going
to write to Ma: so you need n't fret about that. I
wish you'd take my trunk back to Dashville, — I did n't
want to be bothered with it, travelling. I had a bang-
up time at the camp. I'm much obliged to you for
taking me. I like the cadets first-rate, and I shall
join them in the fall. You can tell Ma that I have gone
to take views. You know there ain't any views around
Dashville worth a cent. Tell her she need n't go and
get worried about me ; there won't anything happen to
me, — I guess I know how to take care of myself; and
I shall come home just as quick as I use up my plates.
                    Yours truly,
                              BEN BRADY.

Poor Lieutenant Jones turned pale, and stared
at the letter in blank amazement, as if it could
not be true. What could he say to Mrs. Brady,
and how could he ever make her believe that he
was not to blame ? He thought for a moment of
pursuing Ben, of writing, of telegraphing; but he
soon saw it would be of no use, for there was no

address to the letter, and there was no way of finding out his whereabouts.

But we must leave the unhappy lieutenant to go back to Dashville and break the news of Ben's sudden and unexpected departure as best he could to Mrs. Brady, while we follow the footsteps of "Our Special Artist."

Ben was not in the first class in geography in the Dashville High School, and his knowledge of that branch of learning was as uncertain as his spelling. He had a very vague notion that Virginia was somewhere down South; but how to get to it, he did n't know at all. By dint of inquiring, however, he found out that he must go through New York, Baltimore, and Washington. In one of these places he thought he could get some of the magic liquid with which to develop his plates.

But he had never been in a big city in his life; and when he got to New York, the tremendous crowds of people, the rush, the confusion, the tumult, so impressed him that he dared only go from one depot to the other, and even then was quaking in his boots lest he should be lost.

At the ticket-office in New York there was a man standing close by when Ben went up to buy his ticket for Washington. Perhaps to impress the stranger with his importance and teach him that he must not always judge people by their size, Ben, with a little flourish, pulled out the roll of bank-bills which he had received from his

sitters at Camp Bismarck, and made a great show
counting out his fare. When he took his seat on
the train, he found the same man on the seat
behind him. He turned out to be a pleasant, soft-
spoken man, who by and by began to talk to Ben;
and when he learned where he was going, gave
him much good advice, and told him how to go to
Virginia, and what everything would cost, and
many other things. He happened to have a map
in his pocket, and he came over into Ben's seat
and opened his map and took out a pencil, and
showed Ben his road exactly on the map, so that
Ben thought he had learned more geography from
the soft-spoken man in half an hour than he had
ever learned in the Dashville school all his life.
And when, presently, the stranger saw the camera
under the seat and heard what it was, and drew
out from Ben a description of his visit to Camp
Bismarck and the pictures he had taken, not for-
getting the Governor's, the soft-spoken man declared that Ben must be a wonderful boy, — in fact,
the most wonderful boy he had ever known; and
he ventured to predict that there was a chance —
in fact, the greatest probability — of his some
time becoming President of the United States. In
fine, the soft-spoken man had such kind manners
and talked so agreeably that Ben thought he was
the nicest person he had ever met next to the
Governor, and was very sorry to have him go
when he left the train at Baltimore. Nor after-

ward, when Ben got to Washington and found his roll of bank-bills had mysteriously disappeared, when he stood pale and quaking with astonishment and fear at the discovery, it never for a moment occurred to him to connect his loss with the soft-spoken man.

But now what was to be done? He felt in his trousers' pockets in alarm, and found he had still a little silver. He counted it with much anxiety. There was only two dollars and a half. Forced to pay a dollar and a half for his lodging and breakfast, he reached Alexandria next day with only fifty cents in his pocket. This proved to be just enough to pay his fare in the stage that was to take him to Montville, a lovely little place among the mountains which he had heard Lieutenant Wilder describe.

There were several passengers in the stage when it started; but one after another they all got out before it arrived at Montville, save one little girl about Ben's own age. This little girl was directly opposite Ben, and there they sat, bobbing up and down as the stage jolted along, making believe not to look at each other, but all the time wanting to speak. The little girl had a, bright, merry face; she was not exactly pretty, but very good-natured looking; she had laughing blue eyes, a freckled skin, and reddish hair, which was arranged in two long braids, tied up at the ends with bits of blue ribbon. She held in her lap a very large orange, which she played with now and then when she grew tired of tossing her braids and drumming on the window.

All at once the stage gave a tremendous jolt as they passed over one of those queer hummocks in the road which the country people call "thank-you-marms," and away went the orange on the floor. In a minute Ben sprang to pick it up, and the little girl sprang to pick it up; so they met in the middle, and their heads came together with a tremendous bump. Then they both sat back in their seats, and the little girl began to laugh, whereupon Ben blushed and bit his lip. Then the little girl laughed harder than before; she looked out of the window and puckered up her lips, and put her handkerchief up to her mouth, and tried very hard indeed to stop. But all in vain; she presently burst out again, and laughed and laughed till the tears stood in her eyes. By this time Ben had become very indignant; he did not like to be laughed at, — he considered himself a person of altogether too much consequence; so he got up and went across the stage, and turned his back on the little girl and looked out of the other window. Pretty soon, however, he felt a touch on his shoulder, and there was the little girl holding out half of her orange, which she had peeled for him. She did not say anything, but she looked so sorry and so eager to be friends that Ben was mollified, and so took the orange and returned to his seat.

As they sat there eating their oranges and look-ing rather bashful, the little girl, taking courage, suddenly asked, —

"What 's your name ? "

"*Mister* Ben Brady," said Ben, thinking to im-press the little girl with his dignity.

"My name is Sissy Sanderson," she rejoined; "my father 's the town clerk. Everybody knows us."

"Humph!" exclaimed Ben, not very politely, thinking to himself that he was somebody, and he did n't know the Sandersons.

"What 's that thing ? " asked Sissy, pointing to Ben's apparatus, tucked down beside his seat.

"It 's a tourograph!" replied Ben, loftily.

"Oh!" exclaimed Sissy, none the wiser.

Ben gazed out of the window with a proud air, as much as to say, "Look at it now while you have the chance; you don't see a tourograph every day!"

"Do you play on it ? " asked Sissy, again.

"Nobody *plays* on it!" exclaimed Ben, indig-nantly. "I take pictures with it. I am an artist!"

"*You* do!" exclaimed Sissy, almost gasping with astonishment; and then she looked from Ben to the tourograph, and from the tourograph to Ben, for three whole minutes, so overcome with awe and admiration that she could not speak.

"Who taught you ? " at last she asked.

"Nobody; I taught myself," replied Ben, shortly, seeing the effect he had produced on Sissy, and now feeling that he had risen once more to his proper level.

"Where are you going?" asked Sissy, more and more interested in her new acquaintance.

"Going to Montville."

"Why, that's where I live. I know everybody in Montville. Whose house are you going to?"

"I'm not going to anybody's house; going to the hotel," said Ben, haughtily.

"Why, there is n't any hotel," said Sissy.

"Eh!" exclaimed Ben, in alarm.

"Did n't you know the hotel was burned down a long time ago?"

"Wh — wha — what shall I do then?"

The pride and haughtiness faded very suddenly out of Ben's face, and gave place to a look of blank dismay as he felt in his trousers' pockets and found them empty, as he thought of himself hundreds of miles from home, with no means of getting back, and now just about entering a strange town, with no hotel, and the night coming on. He gazed ruefully down upon the tourograph, and then out of the window, and looked very, very crestfallen and forlorn.

"Have n't you any relations in Montville?" inquired Sissy.

"No."

"And don't you know anybody?"

"No."

"Then what made you come here ?"

"'Cause Lieutenant Wilder said there were splendid views here."

"What, Charlie Wilder ?"

"Yes!" cried Ben, brightening up a bit. "Do you know him ?"

"Oh, yes, indeed! he was my sister Molly's partick'ler friend when he was here. He used to come to our house often. How funny you should know *him!*"

There was a few minutes' silence, during which the kind-hearted Sissy was busily thinking, when, suddenly, she exclaimed, —

"Why, I 'll tell you what you can do. You can come to our house to supper, and bring your troorer — two — row — gr —, the *thing*, you know," cried Sissy, in a desperate attempt to remember the name; "and I 'll ask Mother, and *she 'll* find some place where you can go."

Ben blushed a little, and muttered out his thanks rather awkwardly. But he was glad enough to accept the invitation, which took a big load from his heart, as you may believe; and heaving a deep sigh of relief, he cast a look of gratitude at Sissy, and for the first time began talking and laughing with her quite easily. In this way they at length rolled into the pretty village of Montville, where they were presently set down at Mr. Sanderson's door.

Sissy immediately stepped out of the stage and ran away, crying, —

"I'll go and tell Mother you've come."

Pretty soon she came back with her mother, who proved to be a plain, stout, middle-aged woman, with a very pleasant look in her face. They found Ben sitting on the doorstep, looking very dismal. Mrs. Sanderson took him in and welcomed him heartily; and after asking him some questions about Lieutenant Wilder, and looking with much curiosity at his tourograph, of which Sissy had already given her some account in an awed and mysterious whisper, Mrs. Sanderson called in her son Bob, a boy of about the same age as Ben, and bade him show their little guest upstairs, saying kindly, —

"If you are a friend of Lieutenant Wilder's, you must stay with us, my dear, while you remain in Montville."

Then Ben, with another sigh almost as big as he was himself, but with a light heart, followed Bob upstairs.

The next day, bright and early, and every morning for some time afterward, Ben started off in search of views. Up the hills and down the valleys he marched, never getting tired, stopping every now and then to take a picture, and always attended by Sissy and Bob, who were his constant admirers. Sometimes they went with Sissy's donkey-wagon, and sometimes they went with

Bob's team, which was funnier still. Bob's team was nothing more nor less than an ox-cart. That was rather a queer thing for Bob to have; but this is the way it happened. Two or three years before, when Mr. Sanderson was about to send off two young calves to the butcher, Bob begged so hard for them that his father gave them to him, and he had brought them up and trained them and broken them in, till now they were the handsomest pair of steers in the whole country-side. Bob had trained them so that he could sit in the cart and shout "Gee!" and "Haw!" and they would go whichever way he wished. He called one "Jack" and the other "Jill;" and when Sissy laughed at this, and said Jill was a girl, Bob said he did n't care; he liked the name of Jill, and it would do just as well for an animal as it would for a girl.

After Ben had thus photographed all the fine scenes he had heard Lieutenant Wilder describe, he began to take views of the town; and he soon became as well known and famous among the townspeople as he had been in camp. He wore his cap with the badge wherever he went, and was at once an object of envy to all the boys and of admiration to all the girls. Nobody understood very clearly why Ben did n't finish up his pictures; but they listened in good faith to his story of the magic liquid, and as he took good care to tell all about Camp Bismarck, and how he took the

officers, and last of all the Governor himself, they
could n't doubt his word.   Besides, there was the
instrument itself, — there had never been one before in town ; and if it did n't take pictures, what
did it do ?   Again, Ben's experienced air, — for
he had now taken so many pictures that he went
through the operation with great ease and quickness, — all these things tended to impress the public with his knowledge and skill.

Thus he went about the village always attended
by a group of white children, a lot of ragged little
darkies, a few grown-up men who had nothing
better to do, and now and then a stray dog or cat.
He took views of the chief buildings and objects of
interest, — the town-house, the pound, the grocery
store, and the blacksmith's shop.   The poor smith
stood with a horse's foot in his lap, and his heavy
hammer uplifted in the air, waiting, until his
back ached, to be taken.   But as soon as Ben got
ready, then the horse would switch his tail to
brush off a fly, or the smith would have to mind
his bellows, or a pig would run in the way, or
something else happen, which of course was not
Ben's fault.

Then at home he had to take ever so many pictures of the Sanderson family and all their friends.
There was Mrs. Sanderson in her best black silk,
holding a prayer-book in her hand.   There was
Granny Sanderson in her best cap, with her jet-
black front tied on askew.   There was Mr. San-

derson in his Sunday clothes, with his long locks
combed down very straight and smooth, staring
with a stern look at a fly on the wall. There was
Bob, with his hair sticking straight up in the air,
and his eyes looking a little wild. There was
Sissy, with her freckles and braids, smiling help-
lessly, for she protested she never could keep sober
with "that thing" pointed at her. And last, but
by no means least, there was Miss Molly. I say
Miss Molly, for she was a grown-up young lady
and the beauty of the family; and not only that,
but the beauty of the whole town, as everybody
acknowledged. I am sorry to say that people had
noticed Molly's good looks, and silly friends had
told her she was handsome, until she had become
so vain of her beauty that she thought of very
little else. Now, therefore, she was constantly
"posing" to Ben for her picture. And Ben, as
you may suspect, was only too glad to find his ser-
vices in such demand by the belle of Montville.
Accordingly, he took her in all kinds of attitudes,
in which he exerted his utmost skill, and Miss
Molly made frantic attempts to be fascinating.
Now in her big Gainsborough hat, almost as large
round as the top of a barrel; now with her hair
let down and her eyes rolled up like a Madonna;
now wearing a wreath of flowers as "The Bride,"
or veiled with the mosquito-net as "The Spirit of
Light;" now with her head turned to one side,
her hands resting upon a parasol that lay across

9

her lap, and an affected smile upon her face, as
" The Coquette." Our young photographer decided
that this last " would be a very good picture, only
the arms and the parasol were a little out of
focus."

After a time, however, Miss Molly's thoughts
took a tragic turn. She tried attitudes for hours
before the glass; and when she hit upon one that
was fine enough, she would " strike it " and call for
Ben to come at once to take her. Sometimes this
must have been very tedious, if not painful, as
when one day she arrayed herself in a bed-quilt
and stood in the middle of the parlor floor till
nearly exhausted, brandishing the carving-knife,
as Lady Macbeth; and all this time poor Mrs.
Sanderson was waiting for the knife to cut up the
cold meat for dinner, but dared not ask for it, as
Miss Molly insisted if she was disturbed in that
attitude she could never " strike it " again, — which,
I believe, was true enough. Another remarkable
attitude of Miss Molly's was when she put three
rows of paper ruffles around her neck, dressed her
hair in puffs, put on Bob's cap with the brim at
the back, donned Granny's long mourning veil,
and looked sorrowfully down at her feet, as Mary
Queen of Scots. But her grandest and most terrible posture was where she rolled up her sleeve
to the shoulder, and then, seizing in her other hand
a toy snake which Bob found among his old playthings, applied it to her bare arm while she threw

MISS MOLLY AS LADY MACBETH.

back her head and fixed a ferocious glare upon the ceiling. This I hardly need to tell you was "Cleopatra and the Asp." The whole family assembled and stood by in awe-struck and breathless suspense while Ben, with trembling haste, took the picture. No one was quite clear how Cleopatra ought to be dressed; but Molly settled the question by tying on a red cotton handkerchief for a turban, and draping herself in one of the chintz curtains from the parlor. And if anybody had objected that this garb was very like old Aunt Dinah's in the kitchen, it might easily have been answered that no Aunt Dinah nor any other mortal cook was ever seen clutching a toy snake and rolling her eyes in that way.

What worried Ben, however, was that he had no screen, and that the corner of the melodeon, with the kerosene lamp on it, would be sure to show sticking out behind Cleopatra in the picture.

Speaking of Aunt Dinah reminds me of Ben's attempt to photograph her. After all the family had been duly taken, they suddenly thought of Aunt Dinah, and rushed into the kitchen to ask her. She beamed with delight at the suggestion, but said, in a sort of shamefaced way, —

"Laws, honey, yer don't wanter tuk an ole body like me."

"Yes, yes, we do; come, Aunt Dinah! come right along!" shouted all the children in chorus.

"He, he!" chuckled the delighted Aunt Dinah,

beginning to divest herself of her kitchen apron,
"ef y' aint gwine fer to take no 'scuse, s'pose I 'll
jes' hab to be tuk. But go 'long, honey, go long!
I 's comin', I 's comin' sho'; only jes' stoppin' to
find sumfin' to frow ober dis yer noddle."

Sure enough, out came Aunt Dinah presently,
in her best plaid apron and kerchief, a yellow turban on, and her gold ear-rings gleaming in the
sun. Ben seated her on a bench in the garden
among the sunflowers, and she made a first-rate
picture, — much better than Ben had any idea of,
and far finer, after all, than Miss Molly in all her
grand attitudes.

But the moment Aunt Dinah was seated she
began to look grave; she grew, in fact, more and
more solemn as Ben proceeded to "fix things,"
till at length, when all was ready, she had stiffened
into a really formidable grimness.

Presently Ben had everything arranged to his
satisfaction; and coming to the front of the camera,
he said, in a warning tone, and with a grand air
that never failed to strike terror to the heart
of the ignorant sitter, "All ready now; take
care!" and immediately pulled off the little brass
cap.

Aunt Dinah had been looking in another direction, but at these words turned quickly toward the
instrument; and whether startled by Ben's action
or tone, or both combined, it would be impossible
to say, but she suddenly started from her seat and

fled toward the house, looking back over her shoulder with a terrified face as she cried, —

"Run, chil'en! Massy sakes, run! it's gwine to go off! Seed one o' dem yer t'ings bust afore now! Done knock cheryt'ing all to nuffin!"

The children all laughed and shouted at poor Aunt Dinah's fright, but nothing could induce her to go back and have her picture taken.

"Dis ole nigger seed too many dem yer shootin' t'ings in de war," she said, solemnly. "Yo' kin go on ef ye wanter, jes' go right on; but I's tell yer, honey, tell yer sho', dat ar's gwine ter go off one o' dese yer fine days, an' den whar 'll ye be? Whar 'll ye be den?" she repeated, shaking her head warningly. "Won't be nuff o' yer lef' to wipe up de flo'."

Beside the Sandersons, Ben was called upon in due time to take some of the neighbors. His greatest trial, however, was with the Mallory twins. Mrs. Mallory was very fond and proud of the twins, — so extravagantly fond of them that she often said they were good enough to eat. They were as like each other as two peas; indeed, Ben thought they were a good deal more alike than any two peas he had ever seen. They were just one year and two months old. Why Mrs. Mallory was so proud of the twins, except for the fact that there were two of them, nobody was ever able to find out; but she was, and that was enough for Mrs. Mallory, and indeed for Mr. Mallory too,

— they were both very proud of the twins, and the taking of their pictures was a great event in the Mallory family.

The appointed day arrived. Ben was told to come with his instrument at eleven o'clock precisely, for that was the time the twins awoke from their morning naps. He went accordingly. He was shown into the parlor, where the whole family was gathered awaiting him. Ben by this time felt quite experienced. He had taken almost everything else but a baby, and although it was a bold thing to begin with twins, Ben felt pretty sure of himself. Presently the twins were brought in, and straightway there was a chorus of admiring relatives, — "Darlings," "angels," "cherubs," "pets," "lambs," "little dears," etc. Ben did n't join in the chorus; he did n't exactly know what to do, and so only stood and twirled his thumbs and looked foolish. He knew very little about babies, and still less about twins; "but," as he told Sissy privately, "he could n't see anything to make a fuss over; he should a great deal rather have a couple of nice rabbits." They were chubby babies, and it must be confessed that they were not handsome. They were dressed in long white dresses tied up at the shoulders with pink ribbons. They were girls, and their names, which their mother had made it a point to get as nearly alike as possible, were Emeline Anna and Eveline Hannah.

And now there was a great dispute as to how they should be taken. Some thought in the cradle, some thought in the baby-wagon, some thought on their mother's lap, some thought on their father's lap, while their Aunt Jane said they looked "too cunning for anything" in the clothes-basket. But soon Mrs. Mallory settled the question by taking them one on each knee. Now Ben went to work; he pointed his instrument, adjusted his lens, looked under the black cloth, and was just upon the point of saying the word, when suddenly Emeline Anna set up a cry. Three aunts at once rushed to the rescue, which made her cry louder than before. Mrs. Mallory then sent the aunts away, and by some stratagem of her own secured silence. In a few minutes they were all ready to start again, when, unhappily, Eveline Hannah espied the ribbon on a little blue-and-white sock sticking out from under her dress, and directly was seized with a wild desire to clutch it. This endeavor brought the three aunts and the father promptly to the scene. All at once, it occurred to their Aunt Jane that it would be "so sweet" to have them "looking up." Thereupon she went and got the dust-pan, and, standing on a chair behind Ben and the camera, she pounded it with a clothes-pin. This struck Papa Mallory as such a very clever thing to do that he went and got the poker and tongs, and stood on another chair and banged them together. This produced the desired effect. The four eyes were strained upward in a gaze of dumb astonishment.

"Now, quick, quick!" cried everybody.

Ben, in a flutter, pulled off the cap. The whole family stood rigid with suspense for several seconds. Ben at length replaced the cap, crying triumphantly, "Done!" Alas! in another moment he found that, in the confusion and excitement of getting the twins fixed, he had forgotten to put in the plate, and of course there was no picture.

Up went Papa Mallory and up went Aunt Jane on the chairs again, bang went the poker and tongs, and clang went the clothes-pin and the dust-pan. This time, however, the plan did not work. Eveline Hannah suddenly took it into her "precious little head" to be scared at the noise, and at once set up a cry which, when Emeline Anna presently joined in, became a loud and prolonged duet. It was plain that something else must be tried. It was therefore decided to let Papa Mallory hold the twins, while Mamma Mallory amused them. This promised at first to succeed. Mamma Mallory knelt down before the darlings, and clapping her hands, cried softly, —

"Goo — goo! Googly — goo!"

Now, children, I wish I could explain those words to you, but I cannot. I have not the least notion what they mean. But — will you believe

TAKING THE MALLORY TWINS.

it? — the twins did; they knew at once, and burst
into the sweetest smiles of which they were capa-
ble. Everybody again cried, —

"Quick, quick! Take 'em now! Take 'em
now!"

But Ben, squinting under his black cloth, found
he could see nothing at all but Mrs. Mallory's
back hair. "Oh, dear!" she cried, when Ben
told her of this, "if I go away, they'll be sure
to cry!"

But it seemed now as if the twins had exhausted
their ingenuity for the time, and had stopped to
think up something else to do. They puckered
their mouths, and looked pensively at the floor.

"Now," thought Ben, "I'll catch 'em on the
sly!" And so he did. *They* were quiet, *they* sat
still; and neither Ben nor anybody else in the
room noticed that Papa Mallory *had been trotting
each knee gently all the time.* After this utter
failure, Ben gave up the twins in despair.

But although the Mallorys and many of the
other neighbors were very willing to employ Ben,
and even in some cases to order a dozen pictures,
it never seemed to occur to anybody to pay in advance, and Ben had not the courage to demand it.
So, instead of the great fortune he expected to
make, he was not only without a penny, but depending on the kind-hearted Sandersons for his
board. At last, one morning, he made the start
ling discovery that he had used up all his plates.

Now, instead of a millionnaire and a celebrated artist as he had fancied himself when on the way to Virginia, all at once it occurred to him that he was only a boy a very long way from home, and with no means of getting back there. He began, too, to want to see his mother; he even felt like crying a little, and the world looked very, very dark and dismal. Just at this moment Sissy came up, and seeing Ben look so doleful, asked him what was the matter. He told her everything. Thereupon the sensible Sissy said, —

"Well, you ought to go right away and sit down and write your mother a good long letter, and tell her all about it!"

And so Ben did; and his poor mother, who had been nearly distracted with anxiety, sent back an answer at once by telegraph, saying that his cousin, Lieutenant Jones, would come on to Montville immediately to bring him back.

Very much ashamed was Ben to meet his cousin, you may be sure, after all the trouble he had caused, and very silly and guilty he felt, like little boys who play truant from school. Still more ashamed was he to confess that he had been depending all this time on the hospitality of the Sandersons.

However, good, kind Mrs. Sanderson would n't hear of taking a cent from Lieutenant Jones; she said they would be all well repaid when Ben sent them on their pictures which he had taken. Indeed, I think Miss Molly was rather eager to have him go, — she was so anxious to see her pictures.

They arrived at home in two days; and during the journey, Lieutenant Jones, as the mother's spokesman, delivered a severe lecture to our artist. So before the boy saw her again he had come to understand the fright and anxiety he had caused her. And when they met, Ben burst into tears, which told his mother how sorry and ashamed he was better than a thousand words could have done.

Two days after, he got up before sunrise and went to work developing his plates. Eager, curious, trembling with anticipation, he took them one by one into the dark closet and applied the magic liquid. He watched, he waited, he peered through the gloom by the light of his ruby lamp, he scanned each little line and point. What was the matter? Why didn't they come? He took them out to the daylight. He soaked them again and again in the liquid. What did it mean, all these misty, cloudy, confused-looking objects? What was this meant for? And this? Where were the tents, the camp views, the officers? Where, oh, where was the Governor? Where were the beautiful views in Virginia? Where were the Sandersons? Where Miss Molly's "The Coquette," the "Cleopatra," the "Spirit of Light," "Lady Macbeth," and the "Queen of Scots"?

A more dreadful set of pictures was never seen, I am sure, — a more dismal failure never heard of.

What did it mean? Why, it only meant that Ben did n't know how to take pictures; it meant that he did n't make any distinction between working out-doors, where the light is fierce and strong and the picture takes in a second, and in-doors, where the light is weak and the picture does not take in less than a whole minute. It meant that, not having his magic liquid with him, he could not see his mistakes, and so could not learn experience from them. Poor Ben! He was stunned, he was staggered. He leaned up against the wall. Long had he been waiting for the moment of triumph when he should bring forth his views to the light to convince his mother and show all Dashville what a genius he was, to repay all the favors of the cadets, to return the compliment of the Governor, to requite the long-continued hospitality of the Sandersons, and last, — far worse than anything else, — *to earn the money he had taken in advance from the officers!*

It was a great big piece of humble-pie Ben had to eat when he went to tell his mother of his disappointment. He walked up and down his chamber floor a long time before he could gather courage to do it. His mother did not seem at all surprised; but when she went on gravely and told Ben that now she must pay back to the officers the money they had advanced, and pay the Sandersons for his board, and that, in short, with the expense of sending after him to Virginia and everything else, his career as an artist would cost her over a hundred dollars, poor Ben was very much dismayed, and was quite thoughtful and downcast all the rest of the day.

The next morning he got up early and went and tucked his tourograph away in the darkest corner of the garret, and never mentioned it again. That afternoon, as he was standing at the window, he suddenly saw Johnny Townsend come out of his house across the way with his fishing-rod and basket and go down the street. Ben stood a moment struggling with his pride; then he ran out and called, —

"Johnny! John-nee!"

"Wha-a-t?"

"Got bait enough for two?"

"Ye-es."

"Then hold on; I'll go with you — if Ma'll let me!"

VII.

THE TRAMP'S DINNER-PARTY.

VII.

THE TRAMP'S DINNER-PARTY.

"NEW England States cloudy, northeasterly winds, light rains." That was what "Old Probabilities" said, and people ought to have known better than to go out without their umbrellas; but they did n't.

They thought because the sun shone in the morning it was going to shine all day, and that is how I happen to tell this story. For I should not have sat so long at my window overlooking Boston Common if I had not been amused; and I should not have been amused if I had not seen the people running home all dressed in their Sunday toggery, holding up their skirts out of the mud, covering up their hats and bonnets with handkerchiefs and shawls, while the rain wilted their fine flowers and feathers, took the polish from their boots, and ran down in little rills from the ends of their noses.

But there are other sorts of leaves and flowers than those that are stuck upon bonnets, and *they* liked the rain, — it did n't wilt *them;* besides which, old Mother Earth was thirsty and wanted

10

a drink, and she took it, never heeding the silly people who ran scolding home.

And oh, how magical was the effect of that drink! I wish every bright-eyed boy and girl that reads these lines had been standing beside me that Sunday afternoon to see the change that came over the gray old Common in two or three hours. Little waves of greenness seemed fairly to roll over the dead cold ground; starting away down in the southeast corner by the deer-park, where the gentle does were poking their noses through the wire lattice to be fed or caressed, and sweeping up past the old Burying Ground, down around the Smoker's Circle, then up again to the Frog Pond and away over to the Parade Ground, wave following wave, and each one seeming greener than the last.

Then up among the branches another change quite as wonderful had taken place, for suddenly every little twig seemed to bristle with brown and red burgeons, wherein were packed away tightly, as in the trunks and hat-boxes of a Saratoga belle, all the beautiful spring and summer dresses for the coming season, scalloped and frilled and fluted all ready for use.

"But what has all this to do with the Tramp and his Dinner-party?"

Why, not much. It is only what I happened to be thinking of when the Tramp came along.

He came sauntering down the mall in the most

leisurely manner, with his hands in his pockets, without a bit of an umbrella or an overcoat; and that, I suppose, is how I happened to notice him so quickly, — he was so entirely at his ease while every one else was hurrying with might and main. He didn't seem to mind the storm at all; indeed, he looked just as though he didn't know it was raining.

Perhaps he had *his* Sunday suit on too. I never should have known he was a Tramp from his dress. It was his manner that told the story. Without speaking a word, or making a sign, or even seeing me at all, he told me in a very few minutes all these things, —

"I have no friends, I have no home, I have nowhere to go and nothing to do."

He stopped directly opposite my window, and went and sat down on one of the wet iron benches on the mall. He leaned his elbows on his knees and looked at the ground, while the rain pattered fast upon his rounded back, and ran in a little stream from the brim of his slouched hat. He made a desolate looking picture, such as artists often like to paint; but when he sat up, his face did not seem unhappy. On the contrary, he looked quite unconcerned, and putting his hand in his pocket, he pulled out a large piece of bread.

Scarcely had he begun to eat it when a little cock-sparrow came fluttering down from the tree overhead, lit on the ground, perked up his bright

eye and sharp beak, and kept a keen lookout for
a falling crumb. The Tramp broke off a generous
piece and threw him. The hungry little sparrow
chippered out his thanks, and immediately flew
away to give the invitations to the dinner-party,
which I presume the Tramp told him to do, although I couldn't hear it. There were no re-
grets sent, and everybody came on time, — in fact,
came with incredible quickness at such a short
notice.

A half score of plump, social, gossiping little
sparrows ranged themselves around the munificent
Tramp; and before the feast actually began, the
company was increased by two stately pigeons,
who came in full toilet, — purple and white silk,
pink stockings and shoes.

None of the guests were at all stiff or ceremo-
nious, but fell to with the keenest relish as fast as
the viands were served. The repast was simple
but bountiful; the pocket seemed to hold an ex-
haustless store of bread, and the delighted host
served it up as fast as possible.

There were a great many speeches made, some
songs sung, and I have no doubt a great many
jokes cracked; but I was too far off to distinguish
clearly the character of this part of the entertainment. A more social, free-and-easy party
could not be imagined, nor, I am sure, a merrier
circle found in all Boston.

The rain and the wet seat were forgotten; the

needless luxuries of table, drapery, fine plate, and
service ignored.

And thus the friendless, forlorn, homeless Tramp
was able to call about him a gay, cheerful company, who were above all the cold, empty preju-
dices of society, above the idle forms of etiquette,
who recognized as their best friend and brother
him who had a crust and welcome, and sat gladly
down to share it with his guests.

For a second course the Tramp produced from
another pocket a piece of rather dry-looking cake;
but the rain moistened it in a minute, and it is a
sufficient tribute to its quality to say that not a
crumb was left.

No wine was served with this dinner; but, what
was far better and more wholesome, there was a
large bowl of cold, sweet spring rain, formed by
the twisting roots of a neighboring tree, and here
the satisfied guests slaked their thirst.

Then, as their hospitable host rose to go, the
merry company flew after him down the mall,
chirping out their farewell compliments, and
bidding him — let us hope — God-speed in his
wanderings.

VIII.

BLACK BEARD'S LAST STRUGGLE.

A STRAGGLING village built along a side hill overlooking the sea, — a village composed of rude huts thatched with palmetto-boughs, save for one square stone building standing in the midst buttressed by a massive stone wall, on the top of which stood two small cannon defending the entrance: here lived Jack Teach.

"Who was Jack Teach?" He was a terrible fellow, engaged in a terrible business. To tell the truth, Teach was a pirate, — no pirate of fiction either, but a real flesh-and-blood pirate, whose doings are all set down in history. Indeed, he was one of the worst of his kind, to whom the famous Captain Kidd was but a milksop; for Teach had neither mercy nor compunctions. For years he and his lawless band had roamed the Spanish main in their rakish schooners, until he had become the terror of the seas, and merchants and sailors shuddered at his name.

Seizing upon some uninhabited islands in the Southern Atlantic, he established his sway over the crowd of adventurers who flocked to service under his black banner, and soon became known

as the lawless ruler of the Bahamas. Mariners
on their way to the Southern seas trembled when
his low coast-line hove in sight off their starboard
quarter; and woe betide the hapless vessel which
was driven by the winds upon the terrible coral-
reefs which hemmed him in!

It was an afternoon in September, away back in
seventeen hundred and no matter what. A hot south
wind blew up from the Caribbean Sea, swaying the
tall cocoa-nut palms, shaking the scarlet blossoms
from the wide-spreading ponsianas, and wafting
far and wide the sweet perfume of the orange-trees.
Lizards sported hither and thither over the blank
white wall (made of huge blocks cut from the coral-
reef) which defended Teach's mimic fortress, long
sinuous centipedes peeped from the crevices, while
velvet tarantulas lurked above amidst the big
bunches of golden bananas.

None of these things heeded Jack Teach as he
sat lolling among his followers beneath a huge
silk-cotton-tree which stood half way between his
house and the shore, and afforded by its dense
shade a favorite rallying-place for Jack and his
band. Jack looked like the desperado that he
was. His heavy features were lighted up by a
pair of fierce black eyes, which glared forth from
under his shaggy brows; his red shirt was thrown
open in front, showing his massive throat and
brawny chest; big hoops of gold dangled from his
coarse ears, while his lower face was densely cov-

ered by an enormous beard, from which he received
his nickname of "Black Beard," and which, to
heighten the ferocity of his appearance, he used to
braid and twist up into little tails which stuck
out in every direction.

When in action it is said he looked more ferocious still, in fact, like "a complete fury, with
three braces of pistols in holsters flung over his
shoulders like bandoleers, and lighted matches
under his hat sticking out over each of his ears."

After this description no one will be surprised
to hear that Black Beard had a wonderful control
over his band, the secret of which lay in the fact
that he outdid them all in cruelty and barbarity.
He was even more formidable in his merry moods
than in his wrath. He played extraordinary
pranks, endangering his own life as well as those
of his followers. On one occasion, we are told by
his biographer, "he collected a quantity of sulphur
and combustible materials between the decks of
his vessel, where, kindling a flame and shutting
down the hatches upon his crew, he involved himself with them literally in fire and brimstone.
With oaths and frantic gestures he then acted the
part of the devil, as little affected by the smoke as
if he had been born in the infernal regions, till
his companions nearly suffocated." At another
time we read that "in one of his ecstasies, while
heated with liquor and sitting in his cabin, he
took a pistol in each hand; then cocking them

under the table, blew out the candles, and crossing his hands, fired on each side on his companions, one of whom received a shot which maimed him for life."

But let no boy for an instant be tempted into . admiring Jack Teach; he was a big, coarse, ruffianly bully, and much more like a wild beast than a human being. In fact, he was hunted down like a wild beast at the end, and came to a deserved and ignominious death.

But now let us get back to our story, which, like a great many other stories told of Black Beard, may or may not be true, for we do not vouch for it; we could not if we would, and we would not if we could. The main point is that it might have been true, and so here it is for you.

We left Black Beard and his band sitting under the silk-cotton-tree. Ah! but that same tree was even more remarkable than the man it shaded. Here is a picture of it; and if it be not, as is said, the very same tree that Black Beard sat under, be assured it is as like it as two peas in a pod.

It was a dull time for Black Beard; he had been several weeks ashore, recovering from a wound received in his last engagement. He was thoroughly tired and bored with shore life; there were no people to rob and murder, and no excitement, save cursing his followers or knocking down his slaves, and so he yawned and stretched and groaned alternately, varying the monotony of the hour by

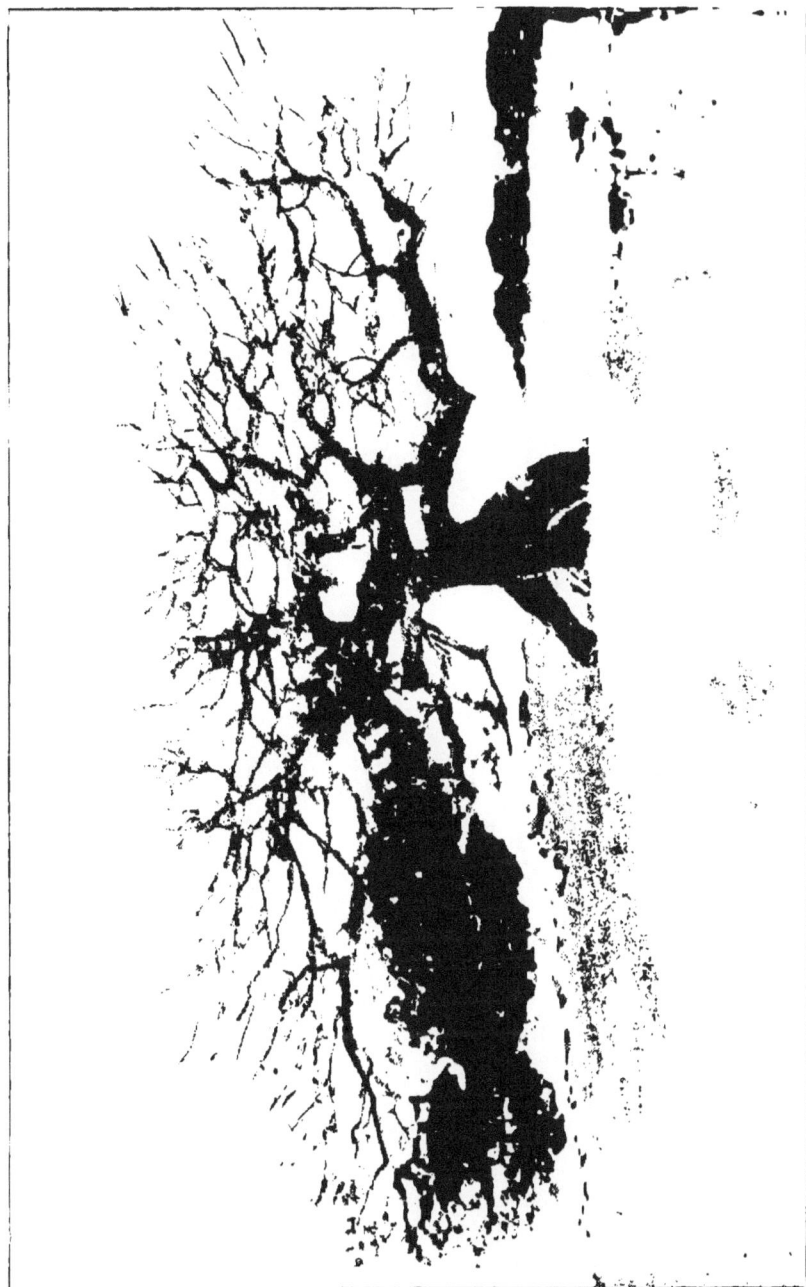

occasionally flinging his heavy drinking mug at the head of the negro who had neglected to keep it replenished, or. calling on one of his boozy companions for a song.

Suddenly the whole gang was aroused by the discharge of a cannon in the direction of the harbor. With one accord they all sprang to their feet and hurried to the shore, cocking their pistols and drawing their cutlasses as they went.

Arrived, they beheld just outside the bar which defended the approach to their shallow harbor the masts of two vessels, the one a small schooner, the other a big merchantman.

"José! José!" cried several voices. "Ay, and with a prize!"

"Huzzah!"

The air was straightway rent with cheers of welcome to their victorious comrade.

"Go give him a salute, can't ye?" cried Black Beard, as a boat was seen to put off from the schooner and head for the shore.

Directly two or three men flew away to discharge the two cannon, while their leader, examining the approaching boat-load through a glass, muttered, —

"Bully José! he is worth the whole crew o' ye put together; he earns his bread, while you lazy dogs are wasting time ashore."

The report of the cannon brought out a half score more of the freebooters from the huts in the village, together with a motley group of half-naked negro slaves, who all hastened to join the crowd gathered to welcome the new-comers.

Much to the astonishment of the assembled throng, when the boat touched shore the officer in command — a burly, low-browed man — lifted out a little girl having a fair, frank English face and a profusion of golden hair hanging in curls about her shoulders, and pointing at Black Beard said, with a grin, —

"There! there he is for ye! go tell him now for yourself!"

Walking directly up to the pirate chief, and fixing her clear blue eyes fearlessly upon him, the child asked, with some asperity, —

"Are you Mr. Black Beard?"

Staring with astonishment at so unusual a visitor, Black Beard nodded mechanically.

"Then," continued the little girl, promptly, "you are a bad, wicked man!"

Instead of taking offence at this reprobation, the pirate seemed to construe it as a compliment; for he burst into a loud guffaw, in which he was presently joined by the whole attendant crowd.

"What 's the matter wi' me, little gal?" asked Black Beard when he had recovered his breath.

"You sent that wicked man there," pointing to the officer who had brought her, "to take my papa's ship, an' he fired guns at us, an' never minded when my papa told him to stop; an' he

"ARE YOU MR. BLACK BEARD?"

threw all the poor crew into the water an' left
them to be drowned, an' he took my papa and
Graham, the mate, an' put big iron things on
their hands an' feet; an' when I told him he must
not, he said you sent him to do it, an' that you
are the one!"

"He told ye that, did he?" said Black Beard,
with a look of amusement.

"Yes, he did; an' he said you would cut off his
head 'less he did just what you told him."

"Lies, lies, little gal; all lies! He's a bad
man that one is; he does all these bad things an'
puts the blame on me, d'ye see? Now," continued
the freebooter, with a wink at his followers, "I
am a good man; I am 'most fit to be an angel,
I am."

At this pleasantry the crowd laughed im-
moderately.

"Then," continued the child, casting upon the
hilarious throng a look of lofty severity, "if you
are a good man, you will make him take those
iron things off papa and Graham."

"Them fellers yonder in the boat?"

"They're not 'fellers;' 't is my papa and
Graham."

"Humph! so? Come here an' kiss me, sweety,
an' we'll talk about it!"

"No, I will not kiss you!"

"Eh? An' why not?"

"Because I don't like your looks."

"My looks!" echoed Black Beard, more and more diverted by the child's talk, "my looks! Why, my dear, I'm considered a great beauty, I am. Take a look at me now," he concluded, pulling off his three-cornered hat, and shaking out his big beard, as a lion might shake its mane. "Ye'll get to like my looks by an' by, an' when ye grow up ye shall be my wife."

The child answered only by a look of disdain.

"What say ye to that?"

"I never would marry such an ugly, wicked old man," returned the child, emphatically.

"Ho, ho!" shouted the pirate, who seemed to enjoy this fearless defiance, as an epicure delights in a piquant sauce. "Ye'll change yer mind by an' by; ye'll come round after a little, never fear. I'm irresistible to the fair sex. But we'll talk about that another time!"

Then, suddenly changing his manner, he called on the waiting lieutenant, with an air of authority, for an account of his trip. This was rendered in a jargon of mixed Spanish and English quite unintelligible to the child, who stood by listening with closest attention.

"And the crew?"

"They'll tell no tales," with a dark look of significance.

"What prisoners?"

"Yender — captain an' mate — in irons," pointing to the boat.

" Ransoms ? "

José nodded.

" Bring 'em here ! "

Thereupon the two prisoners were brought, manacled, before the pirate chief.

"So you're the captain," said Black Beard, gruffly, surveying his principal prisoner coolly from head to foot. " We generally kill fellers like you; but if they have friends to come down with the rhino, we give 'em a chance. So now, what d'ye say ? "

Incensed by this impudent demand, the captain of the captured ship answered indignantly, —

" I say you're a miserable robber and cut-throat, and ye 'll get no ransom out o' me."

"Dog!" cried Black Beard, with a volley of oaths, "dare ye wag yer tongue like that at me ? " advancing at the same time in a threatening way upon his prisoner.

"Dare I ! " cried Captain Wilson, drawing himself up in an attitude of defiance; "if I had free hands and a fair field you 'd see what I 'd dare, you cowardly bully ! "

Flaming with passion, Black Beard flew upon the helpless, manacled man, and striking him a tremendous blow, felled him senseless to the ground.

" Take the carcase away ! " he roared to his followers; "and if he ain't dead yet, put an end to him."

With a loud cry of grief and horror the child threw herself upon her father's bosom, and the two were carried away just as the other prisoner was brought up.

It was an unhappy moment; Black Beard was in a furious rage, and at sight of Mate Graham he broke forth with an oath, —

"Another! Blow out his brains an' bury the two together. Off with him! off with him, I say!"

The least sign of fear or weakness would have been fatal to the prisoner; but Graham was a cool man, and a shrewd man too. Instead of flying into a passion like his captain, he answered calmly, —

"Ah! but ye might do a deal better than that, me friend!"

"Eh?" growled Black Beard.

"Captain Wilson yonder is 'ot-'eaded; 'e is vexed to lose 'is ship, poor man, an' wot wonder! But 'e 'as rich friends, an' plenty o' them at that, an' they'd pay a pretty penny, I'll be bound, to get 'im safe out o' this, — 'im an' little Fanny there."

His greed aroused, the pirate's angry brows relaxed, and he lent a reluctant ear to the mate's plea.

"But," continued Graham, with the same quiet voice and manner, "'e's a stubborn one is the captain, — 'e'ud never in the world write a letter 'ome by 'imself, mind ye; 'e'd never suffer a

penny o' ransom to be paid on haccount o' 'im, if
'e could 'elp it, d 'ye see ? "

"What then ? " growled Black Beard, with dark-
ening brows.

"'Then!' w'y wot 's to 'inder me writin' the
letters and tellin' the plight we 're in 'ere? You
put it in the 'ands o' some safe parties on shore
to manage, an' the 'ole thing could be quietly and
comfortably harranged, d' ye see ? "

Black Beard listened and was convinced. Un-
consciously to himself, he thereby assented to and
helped on a plan which was to end in his own
destruction.

The letter to Captain Wilson's family and
friends was promptly written and submitted to
Black Beard's inspection. It is inserted here, that
you may judge of Graham's shrewdness for
yourselves.

To the Friends and Relations of Captain Wilson :

This is written in be'alf of the Captain, who, I regret to say, is at this present moment in most un'appy
straits. To make short of a long matter, I may say 'is
ship 'as fallen into the 'ands of certain gentlemen of the
sea who are hengaged in business strictly on their own
haccount, and who by a very uncomfortable, but it may
be necessary, law of their business 'ave decided that
the Captain an' dear little Fanny, who are now in close
confinement, must be put out of the way, — which means
that they — er — may be, or rather more properly *will*,
be most certainly deprived of their lives, unless on or

before the first day of February next hensuin, the sum
of ten thousand pounds be not forthcoming.

Furthermore, I regret exceedingly to hadd that there
can be no doubt that these gentlemen are in earnest,
an' will most assuredly hexecute this little threat, which
is quite in the line of their peculiar business. Where-
fore I beg and pray all who regard the welfare an' safety
of the Captain an' little Fanny to promptly set about
raisin' this trivial sum and pay it hover without loss of
time to the parties herein to be mentioned, and haccord-
ing to the conditions stipulated in the slip of paper
which will be found annexed. That there may be no
doubt of the urgency or authenticity of this, I may say
that I served under Captain Wilson as first mate in his
late voyage, that I am permitted to write this letter as
a great favor by the pi — er — the gentlemen above
mentioned, and that I hereby subscribe myself, with
great respect,

Your most obedient, humble serv't,

THOMAS GRAHAM.

This letter in some inscrutable way was promptly
despatched to the mainland; and meantime Black
Beard's wrath having cooled, he inquired after the
condition of Captain Wilson, and hearing that he
was already recovering from the effects of the blow
dealt him, gave orders that he should be closely
confined as a punishment for his contumacy; but
as there was no danger of escape, the other prisoners, Graham and Fanny, should be suffered to go
at large.

The mate showed himself so contented and was

on all occasions so quiet and well-behaved that
he became quite a favorite with the freebooters,
and they intimated more than once that he
might, if he chose, become one of them. Far
from expressing any disgust at this proposal,
Graham affected to be moved at such a mark
of esteem, and to take it seriously into con-
sideration.

Once or twice in his straits for entertainment
Black Beard sent for Fanny to come and see
him; but she always firmly declined. The pirate,
however, was not used to having his orders
disobeyed, and thereupon he had her brought by
force.

"Look ye here, little gal," he said, when she
came before him, "everybody on this island does
what I tell 'em; and when I send for you I want
ye to come, mind that!"

Fanny, who had been a spoiled child all her life,
— much of which, since her mother's death, had
been passed on her father's ship, where she had
been suffered to have her own sweet will quite as
much as the pirate, — answered promptly, —

"I don't care what people on this island do, *I*
sha'n't come when you send for me!"

"Eh, ye will not?" retorted Black Beard, putting on a terrible look, and with the evident purpose of frightening his little prisoner, drawing a
pistol from his belt, he fired it several times over
her head and on either side of her.

"I am not afraid of a pistol," said Fanny, disdainfully; "I can fire a pistol myself."

"Can ye so?" said the pirate, dissembling a look of surprise. "Try yer hand at that, then!" handing over, as he spoke, a heavy pistol from his holster.

Fanny took the weapon, and discharged it without a tremor.

"Bravo!" cried Black Beard, in admiration. "I will make ye captain of a privateer when ye grow up!"

"No you won't, for I shall not stay here to grow up."

"And how are ye goin' to get away?" asked the freebooter, triumphantly.

"The King will send a big ship and blow up all your little ships and take me away by and by, my papa says so," says Fanny, edging away as she spoke.

"Ho! ho!" laughed Black Beard, scornfully, "the King has tried that game before; the King has not a ship big enough to do that little job. But sit ye down here, little gal, I want to talk with ye!"

"No," said Fanny, emphatically, "I won't talk to you; you keep my poor papa a prisoner, and you are a bad, wicked man!"

Black Beard, about to answer, was called away to settle some dispute among his followers, and Fanny took advantage of the interruption to withdraw.

Meantime, the sly Graham had been laying a plot to escape from the island. Noticing a small sloop in the harbor which seemed, from her appearance, a good sailer, he bribed the negro slave in whose hut he was quartered to help him convey on board provisions for a few days' voyage, and promising the slave his freedom if he would accompany him, one dark night when the pirates were having a carouse in Black Beard's house he managed to slip out of the harbor unobserved, and before his absence was noted was far out of sight on his way to the Carolinas.

The pirates cursed and swore and made a great to do when they discovered that the crafty Graham had given them the slip; but they thought the poor mate of a merchantman was not worth pursuing, and so let him go, thus making, as will presently appear, a sad mistake.

Weeks and weeks went by, affairs on the island remained much in the same state, the seasons came and went, and brought no change. Eternal summer breathes around that favored spot, where the flowers bloom and the fruits ripen all through the livelong year.

Black Beard with all his principal followers, in one of his swiftest vessels, had gone off on a marauding expedition along the coast of the United States, leaving orders that nobody should quit the island during his absence, and that a strict guard should be kept upon Captain Wilson and his daughter.

Meantime it behooves us to see what became of the adventurous Graham. Having safely reached the United States, he lost no time in reporting the capture of Captain Wilson to the Governor of North Carolina, and begging that some speedy measures should be taken for his release. The Governor, however, having no force at his command adequate to such an undertaking, despatched the zealous mate to Virginia in a coasting-vessel then about to sail, with credentials to the authorities there.

After a quick passage to Richmond, Graham sought out the Governor, made such a forcible presentation of his case, and was able, moreover, to furnish such a clear statement of the number and force of the pirates and the resources of their island stronghold that his Excellency determined once and for all to send out a strong force for the destruction of the freebooters who for so many years had been the terror and pest of the seas.

Accordingly, as soon as might be he fitted out two stanch sloops under command of a certain brave Lieutenant Maynard, with orders to pursue and exterminate the dreaded Black Beard and his lawless gang at whatever cost of money and of life.

Thus it chanced one stormy afternoon in November, as Black Beard was busy in his marauding work among the creeks and shallows of an inlet near Cape Hatteras, word came to him of the approach of the two sloops of war. I may best

tell what followed in the very words of the histo-
rian of the pirate's exploits: —

"The sudden appearance of an enemy preparing
to attack him occasioned some surprise; but his
sloop mounting several guns and being manned by
twenty-five of his desperate followers, he determined to make a resolute defence; and having prepared his vessel over night for action, he sat down
to his bottle, stimulating his spirits to that pitch
of frenzy by which only he could rescue himself in
a contest for his life. The navigation of the inlet
was so difficult that Maynard's sloops were repeat-
edly grounded in their approach; and the pirate,
with his experience of the soundings, possessed
considerable advantage in manœuvring, which
enabled him for some time to maintain a running
fight. His vessel, however, in her turn having
at length grounded, and the close engagement becoming now inevitable, he reserved her guns to
pour a destructive fire on the sloops as they advanced to board him. This he so successfully
executed that twenty-nine of Maynard's small
number were either killed or wounded by the first
broadside, and one of the sloops for a time [was]
disabled. But notwithstanding this severe loss,
the Lieutenant persevered in his resolution to
grapple with the enemy or perish in the attempt.
Observing that his own sloop, which was still fit
for action, drew more water than the pirate's, he
ordered all her ballast to be thrown out, and

directing his men to conceal themselves between decks, took the helm in person and steered directly on board of his antagonist, who continued inextricably fixed on the shoal. This desperate wretch, previously aware of his danger, and determined never to expiate his crime in the hands of Justice, had posted one of his banditti with a lighted match over his powder-magazine to blow up his vessel in the last extremity. Luckily, in this design he was disappointed in his own ardor and want of circumspection; for as Maynard having begun the encounter at close quarters by throwing upon his antagonist a number of hand-grenades of his own composition which produced only a thick smoke, and conceiving that from their destructive agency the sloop's deck had been completely cleared, he leaped over her bows, followed by twelve of his men, and advanced upon the Lieutenant, who was the only person then in view. But the men instantly springing up to the relief of their commander, who was now furiously beset and in imminent danger of his life, a violent contest ensued. Black Beard, after seeing the greater part of his men destroyed at his side, and having himself received repeated wounds, at length stepping back to cock a pistol, fainted with the loss of blood and expired on the spot."

With the death of Black Beard the spirit and prestige of the pirates vanished into thin air. A sufficient force under the guidance of Graham was

straightway despatched to the Bahamas, where
sailing unexpectedly into the little harbor, they
took the robber stronghold completely by surprise,
and quickly overpowered the feeble force left to
defend it.

While the others were engaged in securing the
captives, the faithful Graham, with a couple of men
at his heels, hastened to the place where Captain
Wilson was imprisoned. Knocking down the
guards, they burst open the doors, and bringing the
bewildered captive forth to the sweet outer air and
life-giving sunshine, struck off his fetters and set
him upon his feet. Enfeebled, however, by long
confinement and ill-treatment, he sank down in
a nerveless state to the ground. As soon as he
recovered his presence of mind after such a joyous
surprise, he demanded news of his daughter. By
command of Black Beard, they had been separated
on the pirate's departure, to punish both for their
long-continued contumacy. An instant search was
made for Fanny, and after a long time she was
discovered in a hut on the outskirts of the village,
under the charge of an ill-tempered old crone of
a negress, who to tame her high spirit and complete her subordination had cut off her abundant
hair, confined her in a dark room, and half starved
her, so that she was scarcely recognizable as the
beautiful child who a few months before had
landed upon the island.

When aroused by the disturbance at the outer

door, she ventured to peep forth from her room, and beheld the mate roughly thrusting the old negress aside. With a joyous cry she sprang into his arms, saying, —

"Oh! you good, good Graham, I knew you would come back!"

IX.

A CRUISE IN A SOAP–BUBBLE.

IX.

A CRUISE IN A SOAP-BUBBLE.

PART I.

ONE-DIMENSION SPACE.

WHETHER the mouse ever really did run up the clock or not, I do not know; all I can say is, if she did, 't was of course merely to see the time, and Mother Goose has made altogether too much talk about it.

If it had not been for this talk, the boys would never have had such outlandish names. Their father and mother — good Mr. and Mrs. Dock — had christened them William and Henry, as the parish register would testify; yet, despite this fact, nobody in all Charmington, where they lived, ever thought of calling them anything but Hickory and Dickory Dock.

The boys themselves cared not a fig; they answered to the names without question, and so when, one afternoon, Hickory shouted from the bottom of the stairs, "Come on, Dickory! mother says we can go!" his younger brother never stopped to think what name he was called, but sprang up, dropped his book, clapped on his ragged straw hat, slid down the balusters, and landing at the front door beside his brother, cried breathlessly, —

"All right; come on! You get the towels, and I 'll bring the soap!" Dickory always carried a huge piece of soap to make *foam,* as he called it, in the water.

He knew in a minute what Hickory meant: they were going to the brook to swim. Their mother usually let them go every day when the weather was fine, for the brook was quite near the house, the water was not deep, and, as she often said, nothing could possibly happen to them.

It was a hot, sultry afternoon; scarcely a breath of wind swayed the tall meadow-grass as they trudged along. The cows looked lazily at them from the shade of the chestnut-trees, and the very brook rippled and gurgled drowsily in the bright sunlight. The boys were in high glee. They stripped off their clothes and hung them on the alder-bushes; they ran and bounded over the green banks, plunged into the sparkling pool, pelted each other with tiny pebbles, lashed the water with osier switches, and dived after the fleeting minnows, until one would have thought they were veritable water-sprites instead of flesh-and-blood boys.

Suddenly Dickory bethought him of his soap. He ran up the bank to get it, and straightway set to dashing and splashing it about in the water, until he was surrounded with white, foamy lather. In fact, he had made soap-suds of the whole brook.

"Hurrah! hurrah!" cried Hickory. "I'll tell you what to do: we can make soap-bubbles;" and diving into the bushes, he presently came forth with a long hollow reed, one end of which he thrust into the water, and began to blow through the other.

Sure enough, the next minute a huge soap-bubble rose from the foamy brook. Both boys cried out with wonder and admiration. Hickory kept on blowing bubble after bubble, until Dickory stood in the middle of the brook quite surrounded by big globes glowing with all the colors of the rainbow. He was enchanted; he dared not stir lest he should break them and destroy the fairy spectacle.

"Now," said Hickory, "I am going to take in a long, long breath, and blow a tremendous one right in the middle."

"Stop, stop!" cried Dickory. "You can't; that's where I'm standing; there isn't room here; you'll break all the others!"

But Hickory would not heed him; he plunged the reed deeper down into the water, shut his eyes, puffed out his cheeks, and blew with all his might and main.

"Stop! There, there, see what you're doing!

12

Why, what's the matter? I — I can't see you. Where — where are you? Hickory! Hick-o-ry!"

Poor Dickory! those were the last words he could utter. Terror and astonishment made him dumb. A film floated before his eyes, spread all around him, and mounting aloft, closed above his head. He did not realize what was happening until it was too late, until he found himself cased in a gigantic soap-bubble, which, rising from the earth like a balloon, soared away through the air.

Through the filmy, transparent sides of his vapory prison he could see, far below him, the green meadows and the babbling brook, looking now like a silver thread, and Hickory standing there with his hands upraised, growing smaller and smaller every minute, until he became a mere speck and then vanished altogether.

Now above, around, below, there was nothing to be seen; he seemed to be sailing through an airy sea in his crystalline ship.

When he came fairly to realize his situation, he was almost beside himself with grief and fright. He wept and wept and called for his mother and father and Hickory, until from sheer exhaustion he could cry no more. Then, crouching down in the bottom of his aerial vessel, he grew calmer and began to wonder what was going to become of him.

Presently he found himself surrounded by large fleecy objects, which he soon perceived to be

clouds. Anon these began to glow with magnifi-
cent colors, — crimson and purple and gold, — and
then he knew the sun must be setting; but all
the time up, up he flew, far beyond the clouds,
while the sky grew every moment darker, until he
could hardly see.

By and by a light began to shine from behind.
It became brighter and brighter. Turning to see
whence it came, Dickory beheld, to his inexpres-
sible terror, a monstrous blazing ball of fire which
seemed to be coming directly towards him. He
knew at once it must be the moon; and he thought
he was surely going to float straight into it and
be burned up. After a while, however, he saw that
it was still an immense distance away, and he
grew calm again.

A long, long time now elapsed, during which
Dickory kept speeding on his way; and the moon
meanwhile, after circling around him, began to go
down, down, down, until it sank quite out of sight,
and Dickory thought it must have dropped into
the sea.

But he was not left long to ponder that question,
when his attention was drawn to the stars. Now
that the moon was gone, they shone out magnifi-
cently. Dickory had no idea before how big and
bright they were. There was the glittering
Northern Crown set thick with gems, the gigantic Great Bear with his splendid tail, the golden
Lyre, the monstrous Dragon coiled in and out

among the rest, Berenice's Hair all glittering with diamond-dust, beautiful Cassiopeia reclining in her easy-chair, the shining Eagle with outstretched wings, and Job's Coffin with its gilded nails.

Suddenly, while Dickory was lost in wonder at these marvellous constellations, and all around was dead silence, there came a dreadful, rushing, hissing sound, which filled the whole sky with thundering echoes, and a flaming serpent with a long, long tail streamed through the air so close to Dickory that he sprang up and shrieked with terror.

After it was gone, and he had recovered from his fright, however, Dickory knew what it was. He knew it must have been a shooting-star. His mother had often shown them to him streaming across the sky; but he never thought they could be so terrible as this.

At length, quite worn out with all his fatigue and excitement, Dickory fell asleep. When he awoke, he thought he must have slept for days and days, it seemed so long and long ago since he took the bath in the brook and Hickory blew the soap-bubbles.

Now the clouds, the moon, the stars, and the darkness were all gone. All about him was a golden haze. It was so bright that at first he had to cover his eyes. Still above, below, around, on every side, nothing was to be seen, nothing to be heard. Dickory rose to his feet, stretched the cramp out of his limbs, and thought of his mother's nice breakfast-table and how he should like to be sitting down to it as usual. This remembrance made him hungry; and indeed he was just beginning to wonder how he was ever going to get anything to eat again, when he was startled by seeing the sides of his bubble-car contract as if yielding to some outside pressure. Slowly and steadily they continued to close in upon him, until just as they were about to touch his face — bang! — *there was a loud explosion, and the soap-bubble burst.*

Instead, however, of falling with frightful rapidity through the air, as he expected, Dickory only fell a couple of feet and landed upon a soft greensward. Here he lay for a time in a half-stupor, the golden haze still enveloping him, so that he could see nothing. He listened, however, and heard afar off a murmuring sound which seemed every minute to come nearer and louder. Presently it increased to a shrill tumult.

All at once the haze cleared away. Dickory rubbed his eyes and looked about. He saw himself surrounded by a multitude of tall thin objects. He could not make them out. They looked at first like a forest of very tall knitting-needles; but as they were all in motion, he saw they must be alive. Looking closer, he discovered that they wore clothes, and then he knew they must be living creatures. They appeared, moreover, to be in a state of intense excitement, and steadily approaching him. Looking about for a place of retreat, he saw himself hemmed in on every side by countless multitudes of these strange beings.

He began to be very uncomfortable, and wished himself back in the soap-bubble, when suddenly an exceedingly tall and thin individual, who looked for all the world like a huge exclamation point, stepped forth from the throng and asked in a voice as shrill as a fife, —

"Who are you ? "

"I am a person," said Dickory, with dignity.

"What is that ? "

"I don't know," returned Dickory, much puzzled ; "it's a — a — why, it's just a person, and that's all."

The strange creature went back and consulted with the others, and presently returned, saying, —

"That won't do; you must explain who you are."

"I am Dickory Dock."

"Who gave you leave to come here ? "

"No-o-body," faltered Dickory, who did not like the forbidding aspect of his new acquaintance.

"Well, don't you ever dare do it again!" screamed the indignant Exclamation Point.

"No-o, no-o; please, I won't. I did n't want to. I could n't help it. I told Hickory not to."

A threatening murmur went up from the whole

"WHO ARE YOU?"

multitude, which became fiercer in proportion as Dickory was mild and apologetic. Thereupon Dickory, who had thus far been sitting, became alarmed and rose to his feet. At sight of his bulk the strange people were seized with alarm, and fled to some distance.

But Dickory, who after a moment's reflection concluded that any company was better than none, beckoned and made signs of friendship; and they slowly and cautiously returned.

"Can you tell me the way home?" asked Dickory of the Exclamation Point, when the latter came within hearing.

The stranger shook his head.

"Where is this place?" pursued Dickory.

"This is the great kingdom of Thin Man's Land," squeaked the stranger.

"Are all the people like you?"

"Yes."

"What makes you so queer?"

"Queer!" echoed the Exclamation Point, indignantly, "we're *not* queer; this is the way people ought to look."

Dickory looked down at his own chubby arms and legs, and was puzzled. At length he raised his eyes, and pointing to some tall objects in the distance, asked, —

"What are those things?"

"Those are the palaces of the nobility."

"Houses!" cried Dickory, in astonishment;

"they look like fishing-rods. Can you get into them?"

"Of course," returned the stranger, scornfully.

"This is an awful funny country. What — makes everything so — so thin?"

"This is the land of one dimension."

"Dimension?" repeated Dickory, overawed by such a long word.

"Yes, one *way;* don't you understand? People and things can only grow in one direction, — length. We have no breadth nor thickness here. Our wise men tell us there *are* countries where they have those dimensions. Now we see what they mean. You must be one of those frightful people."

"Eh?"

"Is everybody so swollen up and deformed where you live?" asked the Thin Man.

"I'm not swollen up and deformed!" returned Dickory, indignantly. "Where I live, the people are a good deal bigger than me; I'm only a little boy."

"Horrible!" exclaimed the Thin Man, with a shudder, and he was about to turn away to tell his people, when Dickory plucked up courage to say:

"Can't you give me something to eat, please? I haven't had any breakfast."

"What do you eat?"

"Bread and butter."

"What is that?"

"That? Why, that is food," returned Dickory, staring.

The Thin Man went and spoke with his people, a dozen of whom started off and soon returned with something to eat.

Dickory looked at what they brought in astonishment. There were several kinds of food, but all in the same shape, — in thin little sticks like vermicelli, only a great deal thinner and smaller. Dickory saw the reason of this when he looked at their mouths, which were like little dots. He took the food, however, thankfully enough, and ate it all up in a trice. It was not so much all together as a good mouthful of beefsteak. But while Dickory was thinking how little there was, the Thin Men murmured in astonishment at his enormous appetite. Next they brought him some drink in long hollow straws. It was a kind of sweetened water. Dickory emptied twenty of these straws before his thirst was quenched.

Just then there was a commotion in the crowd; two messengers arrived from the king, who had heard of the coming of the strange visitor, and was on his way to see him. In a few minutes, accordingly, a burst of very shrill music was heard, the crowd set up a chorus of deafening squeaks, and his Majesty arrived.

He was attended by his body-guard, who were the tallest men Dickory had seen yet, and all dressed in red, while the king, who was accounted the handsomest man in his kingdom, was so extremely thin that Dickory could scarcely see him.

His Majesty, however, proved to be very good-natured. He was immensely astonished at Dickory's size, and punched him and poked him in the arms and legs, and asked him a great many questions. He was especially curious to know about the laws and government of the people to whom Dickory belonged; and when the latter said he knew nothing about such things because he was only a little boy, the king's long thin face grew longer still with astonishment.

The end of it all was that the king adopted Dickory as his own guest, and invited him home to the palace. Accordingly, they set out, and after a long walk came to the royal abode, which looked at a distance exactly like a little clump of bean-poles; but Dickory found, on arriving, that it was amply large to accommodate the whole court.

As there was not a house in the kingdom big enough for Dickory to get into, he was obliged to stay out-of-doors. Here, accordingly, his meals were served. Here, too, as the climate was mild, he slept, attended always, however, by a body-guard of soldiers who watched him night and day, lest he should intend any harm.

The first night the king ordered a bed to be taken out in the courtyard for Dickory to sleep on; but it was so very narrow that it proved very much like trying to sleep on a wire, and so after balancing himself upon it and tumbling off again and again, to the great amusement of the king, Dickory gave it up, and after that slept very comfortably upon the ground.

The next day Dickory was introduced to the king's children, the royal princes and princesses. They were about his own age and were not long in getting acquainted.

As soon as they felt at ease with each other, the young Thin Men asked if he knew any games. Dickory suggested ball and marbles and peg-top. They shook their heads and looked curious. Dickory tried to explain, but he found it impossible to make them understand what a ball or a marble was; they had no conception of anything round.

"Why, just like an orange, you know, or an apple, or a cornball."

The Thin Men shook their heads again. Dickory was in despair. He gave up trying to explain to them any further, and begged them to play some games of their own.

Accordingly, they did. The first game they introduced was something like "tag." As Dickory was sure he could beat the little Thin Men at *any* game, his astonishment was great, when he began to run, to find not only that he could not catch them, but that he could not even keep within sight of them. With their long thin legs they ran like deer, — oh, a great deal faster than deer, faster indeed than a steam-locomotive! — leaving poor

Dickory puffing and panting along behind; while the crowd of spectators, including the royal family and the whole court, chirped and applauded.

But the drollest thing they tried was "hide-and-seek." The Thin Men crawled into such little out-of-the-way cracks and chinks and crannies that they could not be found, while as for poor Dickory, alas! there was nothing in the whole kingdom big enough to conceal him. He got behind the tallest trees and the largest buildings; but even there, he stuck out so on each side that he could be seen plainly for miles.

The king and people jeered so lustily at this that Dickory lost his temper. He determined to show them there were things he *could* do, and without stopping to think of the consequences, rushed up to one of the royal buildings, pushed with all his might, and before anybody could interfere, sent it tumbling in ruins to the ground.

Immediately there was the greatest consternation. Wild squeaks of rage arose from the crowd. The royal guard were ordered to advance. The mob, mad with excitement, squealed, "Down with the wretch! Death to the ruffian!" and pressed forward to the attack.

Dickory was terribly frightened; he had not meant to do any harm. He did not wish to anger his new friends, but there was no chance for explanations; and seeing that it was necessary to defend himself, he seized a long piece of timber from the ruined building, and swung it around him with such vigor that the guard dared not approach.

Perceiving his advantage, Dickory in turn advanced upon them and drove them ignominiously from the field. Not wishing to pursue his victory further, however, and fearing to make an enemy of the king, Dickory threw down his weapon, made signs of peace, and begged for an interview with the sovereign.

After some reluctance his request was granted, when Dickory, making a humble apology for the harm he had done, said he was very sorry, but that being enraged by the scoffs and jeers of the crowd, he had not stopped to think.

The monarch good-naturedly accepted the apology, and promised that he should be plagued no more. He thereupon issued an edict that no subject, on pain of death, should henceforth presume to irritate the strange giant.

Furthermore, to show his good-will, the king now took Dickory with him upon all occasions. One day, as they were returning from a pleasure excursion, suddenly a storm came on. To Dickory's astonishment, instead of putting up umbrellas to keep off the rain, the Thin Men began skipping and hopping about in the most extraordinary manner. When he asked what this queer behavior meant, he was told they were *running between the drops*. And sure enough, they all arrived home as dry as a bone, while he was dripping wet.

Then Dickory acknowledged there was some disadvantage in being big. But was he big any longer? Happening to look at himself one day attentively, he was startled to note a perceptible falling-off in his chubby arms and legs. He remembered now that he had felt a queer sensation ever since he arrived in Thin Man's Land of being squeezed. He consulted some of the king's wise men, and learned to his consternation that there was a contracting power in the amosphere, and that it would go on squeezing and pinching him until, in course of time, he would become as thin and "elegant in figure" as the native inhabitants.

But Dickory was by no means elated at this news. He had no wish to become like one of the native inhabitants; on the contrary, he resolved to leave the country without loss of time. One day, as he was pondering how to accomplish it, he raised his eyes and saw one of the wise men coming towards him. The pundit, after a profound salaam, acquainted Dickory that he had come with a message from the king.

Dickory made a low bow. The pundit made another salaam, bumping his head upon the ground, and then went on to speak as follows:

"His gracious Majesty is most grieved to announce that the Illustrious Stranger's visit to

Thin Land, although very agreeable to himself, is the cause of much complaint among his
people."

"What have I done?" stammered Dickory.

"Withered be my tongue that I should say it,"
continued the pundit, scraping his very forehead
in the dust, "but these querulous people say your
presence here is rapidly producing a famine."

"A fam — I? — why?"

"Because, say these churls again, of the vast
quantities of food which you eat."

Poor Dickory, who had felt half-starved ever
since he came, from having so little to eat, made
no reply to this, but let the pundit go on. The
latter then recited a long apology from the king,
to the effect that he was sorry to be compelled to
play so ungracious a part, but that the murmuring
of the populace left him no other course, and he
was obliged to ask his guest to depart.

"Why, that's just what I want to do!" cried
Dickory. "Show me the way, and I'll go at
once!"

"Ah!" returned the pundit, shaking his head,
doubtfully, "that we cannot do; we have no knowledge of your country nor its whereabouts."

"Where *can* I go, then?" asked Dickory.

"The king has already determined; he has
appointed an escort, and provided for all your
wants on the journey. It only remains for you to
say when you will start."

"Start!" repeated Dickory, joyously. "I'll start right away; but where to?"

"*To Card-Board Land!*" returned the pundit, quickly, and immediately withdrew before the astonished Dickory could ask him another question.

PART II.

TWO-DIMENSION SPACE.

"YONDER lies your way; we can go no farther. It is death for a Thin-Man to cross that fatal boundary."

The officer of the royal guard halted and pointed to a steep and rugged path which led up a hillside.

"But — but — where shall I go then?" stammered Dickory.

"Follow that path; you cannot miss it!" squeaked the officer; "'t will be safe enough for *you!*"

"Will it lead me home?" faltered Dickory, loath to take leave of his escort, who seemed like old friends now.

"We do not know," returned the officer. "Our wise men think your home must lie in that direction. That is the land of *two* dimensions; yours is the land of *three*, and should lie next adjoining."

Dickory said no more, but bade the guard adieu, and stood silently watching them as they marched off down the valley. He then threw himself on the ground, and for a time felt very lonesome and homesick. At last, however, plucking up courage, he set forth upon his way. After a toilful climb of half an hour, he reached the top of the hill. Here a thick wall of fog uprose before him. He could not see what lay beyond. He paused aghast. Presently, however, remembering the officer's direction, to follow the path, he boldly entered the fog, and groped his way onward.

Scarcely had he gone two score paces, however, when he stepped plump off the edge of a precipice.

Whizz! Like a flash he was whirled heels over head, and began to fall.

Down, down, down, he went for a very long time! Down, down, down, expecting every minute to strike on his head, and be dashed to pieces. Down, still down, he fell; but instead of going faster and faster every minute, strange to say he went slower and slower. Stranger still, he presently felt firm ground under — it seemed to him it was *over* — his feet; and looking up, or as it seemed to him *down*, saw a bright sky over his head.

Such a turning topsy-turvy of the whole world made him dizzy. He walked along reeling. Another strange thing was the difference in the atmosphere; the pinching pressure he had felt in Thin-Man's-Land was suddenly removed from before and behind, but increased on the sides, until he felt that he was being squeezed between two boards. Pretty soon, however, he became used to all these queer feelings. He rose to reconnoitre. A beautiful landscape lay spread out before him, — on the right, fair green meadows, where cattle were grazing; on the left, high mountains; in the foreground, a highway upon which a very stout man was leisurely walking.

Delighted to see a living creature Dickory darted towards the man to inquire the way home. The stout man, who wore no hat and but a single garment, — a tight-fitting tunic which came to his knees, — turned his eyes, saw Dickory, and uttering a cry, immediately disappeared.

Dickory stared in amazement. He looked about on every side to see what had become of him, when by chance casting his eyes towards the meadow, he saw to his astonishment that many of the cows had also disappeared. While he stood wondering at this, the stout man suddenly came in view again, and again vanished like a flash. In his stead a tall, slender figure ran like a ray of light along the highway.

Dickory straightway gave chase. Away ran the figure, and away ran Dickory. The hills and trees upon the roadside as they came up to them vanished into air. Presently, at a turn in the road, a town came into view, — a beautiful town with fine trees and stately buildings. A broad street ran through the middle.

Down this street ran the figure, and down ran Dickory, at its heels.

A crowd collected. Dickory stopped. The figure stopped too, and turned around. To his amazement, Dickory again beheld the stout man.

In a minute now it was all explained. The mystery was cleared up. The stout man was a creature of two dimensions: he had length and thickness, but no breadth. Looking at him, therefore, in the face, he was as thin as a crack; looking at his profile, he was as fat as an alderman.

It was just so with the cows and the hills, the trees and the houses. Looked at sidewise, they were large and imposing; looked at edgewise, they were hardly visible. Now, too, Dickory understood why the cows and the stout man seemed to have vanished: they had simply turned around. The whole land and everything in it seemed made out of card-board. Hold up a card and look at it sidewise, then edgewise, and you will see what is meant.

The people who now surrounded Dickory were the strangest he had ever seen. On the outskirts of the crowd, where he could see them in profile, they looked like the stout man. Approaching the centre, they grew smaller and smaller, until directly opposite him they seemed to be simply dark lines.

Presently the throng separated, and an important-looking person stepped forward. Dickory afterwards learned that it was the Prime Minister.

"Who are you?" he asked, staring at Dickory.

"Please, I am Dickory Dock."

"Where did you come from?"

"I tumbled down out of Thin-Man's-Land."

"You're not a Thin-Man; how came you there?"

"I went in a soap-bubble."

"What's that?"

"It's a — a big round thing, with nothing in it."

The Prime Minister looked blank.

"Like my head," explained Dickory, anxiously.

There was an explosion of queer little sounds, like chirps and giggles; and several persons in the crowd fell prostrate to the ground.

Instantly all was excitement. The Prime Minister commanded the people to disperse, and calling his train about him, drew Dickory away from the spot.

"Don't you ever dare to do that again!" he said, sternly.

"I? — that? — what?" stammered Dickory.

"Don't you ever dare to make another joke in this country!"

"Joke — why, I didn't make any joke."

"Silence!" exclaimed the Prime Minister, more sternly than before. "Don't dare to deny it! You made a miserable joke, sir, and see the result, — five men lie dead on the ground!"

Seeing that Dickory was quite lost in amazement, the Prime Minister at length explained that it was fatal for his countrymen to laugh.

"A laugh," he said, "broadens the mouth and face, and oftentimes the whole body. Breadth is a violation of the laws of our being. Alas!" he concluded, with a sigh, "we are an unhappy race, doomed to an eternal gravity, and yet cursed with the keenest sense of humor."

Dickory was greatly shocked. At home he never willingly killed a fly, and to be the cause of such a tragedy as this made him tremble. The Prime Minister, however, consoled him by saying that he could not be blamed for what he had not intended, adding that laughter was a very common cause of death in their country, and carried off more people every year than any form of disease. "But," he concluded, "let this be a warning: never attempt to be funny again."

The Prime Minister now set forward, taking Dickory in his train. He informed his young guest that a great queen ruled over the nation, to whom he would shortly present him.

Arrived at court, Dickory was quite overpowered at the extent of the palace. He thought it the grandest structure he had ever seen; but he very soon found out that it was only card-board, like the rest.

The Queen received him very kindly, and being told that Dickory could not see her very well edge-wise, she graciously presented her profile.

Her Majesty, in turn, was full of astonishment at Dickory's appearance, and very curious to hear his history. So, indeed, was everybody else; all the great men of the court assembled to see and talk with him. His age was what most astonished them. They could not believe that a person of his size was young, and would ever grow any larger, until one of the wise men suggested examining his teeth. This at once decided the question.

Thereupon the Queen, who had lately lost a son about Dickory's age, wanted to adopt him for her heir in place of the dead prince; but Dickory complained of the pressure on his sides, and said he should very soon be pinched to death if he remained. He therefore begged she would consult her wise men as to how he should get home.

The Queen accordingly called together all the sages in the land, and laid the question before them.

While they were pondering it, she commanded that the best of care should be taken of Dickory, and everything possible done for his entertainment.

Expeditions were made daily to different parts of the kingdom, to visit objects of interest. It was while returning from one of these pleasure excursions, attended by a numerous company of the most distinguished ladies and gentlemen of the court, that a strange and terrible experience befell them.

They were crossing a wide plain where not a house nor a tree nor any sort of shelter was at hand. Everybody was in holiday mood, talking and laughing gayly, when suddenly the sky darkened, and a breeze blew up from the north-west.

"The wind! the wind!" shrieked the vanguard, rushing back upon the main party.

"The wind! the wind!" The cry ran like wildfire through the company, and every cheek blanched with fear.

"What's the matter?" asked Dickory.

"Lost! — we are all lost!" cried the panic-stricken crowd.

Dickory looked around in amazement upon his terrified companions, some of whom threw themselves on the ground in despair; some started to run home, while others seized hold of him, and clung with the desperate clutch of drowning men.

The cause of their fright soon appeared. The wind, sweeping down upon them in heavy gusts, caught up the hapless Card-Men, and tossed them about like straws. Some it dashed to pieces on the ground; some it whirled aloft in the air; and some it swept away, never to be seen nor heard of again.

Great was the lamentation at court over the loss of so many precious lives. The Prime Minister informed Dickory that the wind was their greatest enemy; that it swept away thousands of people every season; that it uprooted their trees, blew

down their buildings, and was the terror and
scourge of their lives. On this account, great
care was taken to build their houses in secluded
places; and pointing as he spoke to the Queen's
palace, he said that that was the only perfectly
secure building in the country, because it was
built at the foot of a lofty mountain.

The next day Dickory attended the funeral of
those who had been killed. Arrived at the place
of burial he was astonished to find no trace of any
graves, but all the people gathered about a spot in
the ground which shone like burnished gold.

Consulting the Prime Minister, Dickory learned
that there were no graves in the country, and that
the bright spot in the ground was called "The
Gate of the Future," and that it was made of pure
gold. Through this gate," said the Prime Minister, "our departed friends are ushered directly into
the next world."

When the "Gate of the Future" was opened,
Dickory was astonished to see the light shining
through. Going nearer he saw to his horror that
the ground was card-board too, and that a hole
had been simply cut through it, and covered with
the golden gate.

Then a bright idea occurred to Dickory: the
next world must be his own, where he had come
from, and where his home was; and now he understood in a minute where all the card-board toys,
the troops of soldiers, sailors, and statesmen, fine

ladies, and peasant maids, which make up our collection of paper dolls come from; *they are dropped through from Card-Board Land!*

Not long after this there came news one day that a terrible tiger had sprung forth from the jungle, and devoured several people travelling on the highway. The Queen gave orders that a hunting-party should be made up to go and destroy the tiger. The boldest and most experienced hunts-men were chosen for the task. Dickory, who had never seen a tiger-hunt, begged leave to go; and the Prime Minister, after warning him of the danger, and cautioning him to keep at a safe dis-tance, finally gave his consent. Dickory was pro-vided with a sharp sword and a stout bow and arrow; and early one morning he set forth with the huntsmen, attended by horses and dogs and an immense concourse of people.

Arrived at the jungle which skirted one side of the great highway, gongs were beaten, and the dogs were let loose to start the savage beast from his lair.

After some time, as nothing was heard, the huntsmen grew bolder, and some of them ventured to enter the jungle.

Suddenly the most frantic squeaks and shrieks were heard, and the next moment the audacious huntsmen came flying from the jungle, pursued by the tiger, with bloody jaws agape to devour them. The ferocious animal sprang among the

"THE TIGER STRUGGLED VIOLENTLY TO GET CLEAR."

crowd, throwing down horses and riders, and tearing to pieces everybody in his path.

The crowd fled, shrieking, in all directions. The boldest huntsmen took to their heels. Dickory found himself left entirely alone, exposed to the attack of the bloodthirsty monster. The tiger paused a moment to take breath, and then came dashing at him.

But Dickory, as soon as he saw that it was only a card-board tiger, felt no fear, and instead of running stood his ground. He threw away his bow and arrow, however, and picked up a stout stick from the ground.

When the tiger came near, and saw how big and round Dickory was, — so different from the cardboard men, — he stopped and stared, lashing his tail. The crowd, meanwhile, which had paused at a safe distance to witness the encounter, now cried out to Dickory to run or he was a dead man.

But just at that moment Dickory made a strange discovery. The tiger having turned sidewise for a moment, Dickory detected several large holes in his body, where the arrows and darts of the huntsmen had gone clear through. Inspired with a bold purpose, Dickory now marched straight up to the astonished beast, and thrust his long staff through one of these holes. The tiger struggled violently to get clear; but taking both hands, Dickory uplifted the once formidable monster high in the air, and whirled him around and around on the staff, as you would twirl a card on a lead pencil.

Tremendous squeaks and chirps and squeals of joy burst from the people, when they beheld this amazing feat of Dickory. With gongs beating and banners flying, the multitude accompanied him back to the palace. There in presence of the Queen and the whole court Dickory shut the tiger into a large cage where he was afterwards kept as the greatest prize in the royal menagerie.

The fame of Dickory now spread abroad through the land, and people flocked from all parts of the kingdom to see him. Renewed efforts were made by the Queen and the Prime Minister to induce him to stay with them; but he rejected all their entreaties, as he felt more and more anxious every day to get home to his mother and father and Hickory.

The good-hearted Queen, when she saw that her young guest was really homesick for his mother, felt the greatest sympathy for him, and commanded the poor perplexed wise men on pain of death to find some means to secure his speedy return.

In the mean time, something took place which in a minute destroyed all Dickory's popularity. It was a terrible accident, and Dickory was the cause of it; but he was not to blame, as you will see. Nevertheless, it resulted in a serious damage, not only to the Queen, but to the entire nation.

It had often been suggested to Dickory to climb

the high mountain back of the Queen's palace, as from that point — the highest in the realm — a bird's-eye view could be obtained of the whole country. Very few of the natives had ever attempted the feat, as it was considered very dangerous, — the only man who had ever reached the summit having paid the forfeit of his rashness with his life. So many lives, indeed, had been lost in the attempt that at length it had been forbidden by law to climb the mountain. The peril to the natives lay in the fact that on the top of the mountain a strong wind was always found blowing, which catching the bold adventurer, whirled him aloft in the clouds or dashed him in pieces in the abyss.

As Dickory was not subject to this danger, it was thought that *he* might reach the top in safety. After much persuasion, he determined to make the trial. The day was fixed. News of the undertaking having gone abroad, a dense throng of people assembled to witness the experiment.

To Dickory there seemed only one difficulty in the way: he must needs ascend the mountain edgewise, and he had grave doubts about being able to keep his balance.

However, at the appointed time he came forth, attended by the Queen and the whole court, and taking in his hands a long balancing-pole, as he had seen the rope-walkers do at the circus, he started up the dangerous ascent.

Advancing slowly, and choosing his steps with care, all for a time went well. But as he approached the summit the path grew steeper and somewhat slippery. Several times he nearly lost his balance, but thanks to his pole. saved himself from falling.

Up, up he went, higher and higher, until the top was almost gained. The crowd below shouted and cheered. Only a few steps more and he would be there. But stop, what was that? Again it came. To his horror, the mountain itself began to sway. What should he do? He could not go back. He could not go forward. He could not stand still. A violent trembling seized him. He grew dizzy. He lost his balance, and began to totter. Seeing that he was about to fall, he threw away his pole, made a wild jump, reached the summit, and fell heavily forward, clasping the topmost peak in his arms.

The whole mountain trembled, swayed a moment, and then, with a tremendous crash that rang through the length and breadth of the land, fell flat to the ground, carrying Dickory with it; luckily for him, he was upon the upper side!

The whole kingdom felt the shock. A wail arose from the terrified multitude. Men shouted, children cried, and women fainted; a wild tumult prevailed.

Dickory arose, stunned and bruised; he staggered towards the palace. The populace received him with threats and curses. The Prime Minister promptly sent the royal guard to protect and escort him home. The same official then made a speech to the people, explaining that what had happened, although a dire calamity, was not Dickory's fault, for he had undertaken the ascent against his will.

But the people would not be satisfied. The highest mountain in the kingdom, the pride and glory of the nation, had been levelled with the ground; the beautiful palace of the Queen was now left exposed to the fury of the wind, and the next hurricane might sweep it from the earth.

Countless voices cried for vengeance; they demanded the instant expulsion of the dangerous stranger. The Prime Minister could only appease them by promising that their wishes should be complied with.

He then came hurrying to Dickory, and told him that not an hour was to be lost. In a short time the whole nation would be up in arms, and he could not answer for the consequences.

Fortunately, that very day the wise men came with a plan for conveying Dickory home. After much deliberation they had decided that the only possible way was to tie a stout rope around his body and let him down through the "Gate of the Future," until he arrived at the next world, which they concluded must be his home.

The Queen shook her head, and the Prime Minister at first looked doubtful; but Dickory eagerly cried that he was willing and ready to make the experiment, and so at last it was decided upon.

The whole night was passed in preparations. When day broke everything was done. The whole court assembled to witness his departure, which was kept a secret from the people. The Queen and her ladies wept. The Prime Minister embraced him tenderly, and all escorted him to the "Gate of the Future."

Here everything was in readiness, — endless piles of rope, and relays of stout men to work it. Great care had been taken to secure absolute safety. It was, moreover, agreed that if no land was reached before the rope was all played out that Dickory was to be pulled up again.

A little swinging seat had been arranged at the end of the rope, with loops for his arms. Into this, having bid adieu to his friends, Dickory now fastened himself, waved his hand gayly, as a signal to the men, and was forthwith lowered through the hole.

Down — down — down — down — down — down he went, twisting and gyrating through the air, until, as he looked up, the Card-board world appeared like a little speck in the sky.

Down — down — down. Still down, and ever down he sank, until he grew giddy with the circling motion; until he grew drowsy, and gradually nodded off into sleep and unconsciousness.

Suddenly he seemed to bump against something. He felt a sharp tap on his shoulder. He started and opened his eyes, and lo and behold! there was Hickory shaking him by the arm.

"Why don't you come, Lazy Boots? I called you a long time ago. I got almost down there, and had to come way back."

"Eh — what? — where am I?" cried Dickory, starting up and looking around in astonishment.

"Where are you, Goosey? — Ha! — ha! — ha! how funny you look! Why, asleep on the lounge in your own room; and here 's your book fallen down on the floor!" cried Hickory, laughing as he stooped to pick up a copy of Jules Verne's "Voyage to the Moon."

"What do you say? — where is the Prime Minister? Where is — did I dream all that?" cried Dickory, rubbing his eyes, in amazement.

"Yes, and you 're dreaming still. Wake up; hurry, I tell you! I 'm waiting to go."

"Go? — where?"

"To the brook, of course; mother says we may. Come on! I 've got the towels!"

"Yes, yes; I 'll come," cried Dickory, picking up his hat, "but Hickory —"

"What?"

"*I guess we 'd better not take any soap.*"

www.ingramcontent.com/pod-product-compliance
Lightning Source LLC
Chambersburg PA
CBHW030324270326
41926CB00010B/1490